The Impact of Reform Instruction on Student Mathematics Achievement

T0347419

Summarizing data derived from a four-year combined longitudinal/cross-sectional comparative study of the implementation of one standards-based middle school curriculum program, *Mathematics in Context*, this book demonstrates the challenges of conducting comparative longitudinal research in the reality of school life.

The study was designed to answer three questions:

- What is the impact on student performance of the *Mathematics in Context* instructional approach, which differs from most conventional mathematics texts in both content and expected pedagogy?
- How is this impact different from that of traditional instruction on student performance?
- What variables associated with classroom instruction account for variation in student performance?

The researchers examined how student and teacher attrition, various interpretations of commitment, treatment fidelity, and teachers' needs for professional collaboration affected data collection. Variations in the quality of instruction, the opportunity to learn with understanding, and the capacity of schools to support mathematics teaching and learning affected the cultures in which student learning was situated and, therefore, student achievement. These variations highlight the need to study the effects of the culture in which student learning is situated when analyzing the impact of standards-based curricula on student achievement.

The Impact of Reform Instruction on Student Mathematics Achievement is directed to educational researchers interested in curriculum implementation in schools, mathematics educators interested in the effects of using reform curriculum materials in classrooms, evaluators and research methodologists interested in structural modeling and scaling of instructional variables, and educational policy makers concerned about reform efforts.

Thomas A. Romberg is Bascom Professor of Education and Professor Emeritus in the Department of Curriculum and Instruction at the University of Wisconsin–Madison.

Mary C. Shafer is Associate Professor of Mathematics Education in the Department of Mathematical Sciences at Northern Illinois University.

Studies in mathematical thinking and learning
Alan H. Schoenfeld, Series Editor

Artzt/Armour-Thomas/Curcio (Eds.) • *Becoming a Reflective Mathematics Teacher: A Guide for Observation and Self-Assessment*, Second Edition

Baroody/Dowker (Eds.) • *The Development of Arithmetic Concepts and Skills: Constructing Adaptive Expertise*

Boaler • *Experiencing School Mathematics: Traditional and Reform Approaches to Teaching and Their Impact on Student Learning*

Carpenter/Fennema/Romberg (Eds.) • *Rational Numbers: An Integration of Research*

Chazan/Callis/Lehman (Eds.) • *Embracing Reason: Egalitarian Ideals and the Teaching of High School Mathematics*

Cobb/Bauersfeld (Eds.) • *The Emergence of Mathematical Meaning: Interaction in Classroom Cultures*

Cohen • *Teachers' Professional Development and the Elementary Mathematics Classroom: Bringing Understandings to Light*

Clements/Sarama/DiBiase (Eds.) • *Engaging Young Children in Mathematics: Standards for Early Childhood Mathematics Education*

English (Ed.) • *Mathematical and Analogical Reasoning of Young Learners*

English (Ed.) • *Mathematical Reasoning: Analogies, Metaphors, and Images*

Fennema/Nelson (Eds.) • *Mathematics Teachers in Transition*

Fennema/Nelson (Eds.) • *Mathematics Classrooms That Promote Understanding*

Fernandez/Yoshida • *Lesson Study: A Japanese Approach to Improving Mathematics Teaching and Learning*

Kaput/Carraher/Blanton (Eds.) • *Algebra in the Early Grades*

Lajoie • *Reflections on Statistics: Learning, Teaching, and Assessment in Grades K-12*

Lehrer/Chazan (Eds.) • *Designing Learning Environments for Developing Understanding of Geometry and Space*

Ma • *Knowing and Teaching Elementary Mathematics: Teachers' Understanding of Fundamental Mathematics in China and the United States*

Martin • *Mathematics Success and Failure Among African-American Youth: The Roles of Sociohistorical Context, Community Forces, School Influence, and Individual Agency*

Reed • *Word Problems: Research and Curriculum Reform*

Romberg/Fennema/Carpenter (Eds.) • *Integrating Research on the Graphical Representation of Functions*

Romberg/Carpenter/Dremock (Eds.) • *Understanding Mathematics and Science Matters*

Romberg/Shafer • *The Impact of Reform Instruction on Student Mathematics Achievement: An Example of a Summative Evaluation of a Standards-Based Curriculum*

Schliemann/Carraher/Brizuela (Eds.) • *Bringing Out the Algebraic Character of Arithmetic: From Children's Ideas to Classroom Practice*

Schoenfeld (Ed.) • *Mathematical Thinking and Problem Solving*

Senk/Thompson (Eds.) • *Standards-Based School Mathematics Curricula: What Are They? What Do Students Learn?*

Sophian • *The Origins of Mathematical Knowledge in Childhood*

Sternberg/Ben-Zeev (Eds.) • *The Nature of Mathematical Thinking*

Watson • *Statistical Literacy at School: Growth and Goals*

Watson/Mason • *Mathematics as a Constructive Activity: Learners Generating Examples*

Wilcox/Lanier (Eds.) • *Using Assessment to Reshape Mathematics Teaching: A Casebook for Teachers and Teacher Educators, Curriculum and Staff Development Specialists*

Wood/Nelson/Warfield (Eds.) • *Beyond Classical Pedagogy: Teaching Elementary School Mathematics*

Zaskis/Campbell (Eds.) • *Number Theory in Mathematics Education: Perspectives and Prospects*

The Impact of Reform Instruction on Student Mathematics Achievement

An example of a summative evaluation of a standards-based curriculum

Thomas A. Romberg
University of Wisconsin–Madison

Mary C. Shafer
Northern Illinois University

 Routledge
Taylor & Francis Group

NEW YORK AND LONDON

First published 2008
by Routledge
711 Third Avenue, New York, NY 10017

Simultaneously published in the UK
by Routledge
2 Park Square, Milton Park, Abingdon, Oxon OX14 4RN

*Routledge is an imprint of the Taylor & Francis Group,
an informa business*

First issued in paperback 2011

© 2008 Taylor and Francis Group

Typeset in Times by Swales & Willis Ltd, Exeter, Devon

Library of Congress Cataloging in Publication Data
Romberg, Thomas A.
  The impact of reform instruction on student mathematics
  achievement: an example of a summative evaluation of a
  standards-based curriculum / Thomas A. Romberg, Mary C.
  Shafer.
  p. cm. – (Studies in mathematical thinking and learning)
  Includes bibliographical references and index.
  1. Mathematics—Study and teaching—United States—
Evaluation. 2. Mathematical ability—Testing. 3. Academic
achievement—United States—Evaluation. I. Shafer, Mary C.
  II. Title.
  QA13.R637 2008
  510.71′273–dc22   2007050663

ISBN13: 978-0-415-50511-6 (pbk)
ISBN13: 978-0-415-99009-7 (hbk)
ISBN13: 978-0-203-89522-1 (ebk)

Contents

Preface   ix
Acknowledgments   xii

1 Summative evaluation of standards-based curricula   1

2 Proposing to study standards-based
   curriculum implementation   15

3 Setting the foundation: initiation of the study   21

4 Building a culture of support for reform:
   implementation of professional development   27

5 Examining the role of teachers: background,
   instruction, and treatment fidelity   36

6 Linking instruction and student opportunity to
   learn with understanding   49

7 Looking at assessment instruments   56

8 Findings about student achievement, question 1:
   what is the impact of the MiC instructional
   approach on student achievement?   64

9 Findings about student achievement, question 2:
   how is the impact of instruction using MiC
   different from that of conventional instruction
   on student performance?   90

10 Findings about student achievement, question 3:
    what variables associated with classroom
    instruction account for variation in
    student performance?   127

11 What we learned from the research and the
    implications for curriculum evaluations   158

    References   175
    Index   182

Preface

In 1992 the National Science Foundation (NSF) funded several projects to develop new sets of instructional materials that reflected the reform vision of school mathematics espoused by the National Council of Teachers of Mathematics (NCTM, 1989). By the mid 1990s, as these standards-based materials were being published and marketed, government agencies and critics of the new materials began to ask for research-based evidence about improved student performance. Rather than basing judgments about the quality of a curriculum on market research, or an author's claims after one or more trials in a small number of classrooms, large-scale summative evaluations of the curricula were being called for.

We wrote this book both to reflect on the issues surrounding the calls for such large-scale evaluations, and to provide policymakers, critics, and other researchers with an example of what it takes to carry out a summative evaluation of the implementation of one of the standards-based curricula. Under any circumstances, classroom instruction is a complex process, hard to study, and difficult to control. Furthermore, large-scale longitudinal studies rely on the willingness of school administrators and teachers to participate and contribute to the study, are expensive to carry out, and produce a plethora of information that makes analysis and reporting of findings difficult and time consuming. This example is a case study in curricular assessment/evaluation. We believe that there are general lessons to be learned as well as the particulars we report. Those calling for such studies should find that this volume exemplifies the kind of approach they are asking for, and that it demonstrates the kinds of assessments that can be meaningfully done, amidst the complexities of "real world" implementations.

The standards-based curriculum being evaluated was *Mathematics in Context* (National Center for Research in Mathematical Sciences Education & Freudenthal Institute, 1997–1998). These middle school curriculum materials were produced by the National Center for Research in Mathematics Sciences Education at the University of Wisconsin–Madison with the assistance of the Freudenthal Institute at the University of Utrecht in

The Netherlands. Funding for the project was provided by NSF (NSF Grant No. ESI-9054928). The materials were created for American middle schools and field-tested prior to being published in 1997–1998 by Encyclopædia Britannica. The *Mathematics in Context* (MiC) materials consist of 40 curriculum units (10 at each grade level 5–8), a teacher's guide for each unit, including assessment materials, and two sets of supplementary materials. The materials differ from most conventional mathematics texts in both content and expected pedagogy.

In 1995, as the development of the MiC materials was nearing completion, a proposal was submitted to NSF to investigate how teachers were changing their instructional practices in schools using MiC and how such changed practices affected student achievement. Two NSF grants were awarded to the University of Wisconsin–Madison: first, to conduct a three-year summative evaluation of the impact of MiC on student mathematical performance (NSF Grant No. REC-9553889); and second, to analyze the data gathered in that study (NSF Grant No. REC-0087511).[1]

In this book, the initial chapter addresses the pressures to evaluate standards-based curricula. The chapter includes a discussion of summative evaluations as an aspect of curriculum research, the difficulties of using randomized experiments for such evaluations, and the rationale for the use of structural modeling as the basis for such studies.

The next nine chapters draw on the summary monographs and supporting technical reports we prepared for the Longitudinal/Cross-Sectional Study of the Impact of Teaching Mathematics using *Mathematics in Context* on Student Achievement. The eight lengthy monographs and 55 technical reports are available at *http://micimpact.wceruw.org/*. Chapters 2, 3, and 4 cover the rationale for the study, the details of initiating the study, and the importance of professional development for the teachers in the study. Chapters 5, 6, and 7 explain the role of teachers, the use of composite indices for capturing variation in instruction and opportunity to learn mathematics with understanding, and the assessment instruments developed and used in the study. Then, Chapters 8, 9, and 10 report the findings

1 The Longitudinal/Cross-Sectional Study of the Impact of Teaching Mathematics using *Mathematics in Context* on Student Achievement was carried out by the staff of the Wisconsin Center for Education Research, University of Wisconsin–Madison with the support of the National Science Foundation Grant No. REC 0553889. The analysis of the data gathered in this study was conducted by the staff of the Wisconsin Center for Education Research, University of Wisconsin–Madison and funded by the National Science Foundation Grant No. REC 0087511. Additional support for completing the monograph series was provided by Northern Illinois University. Any opinions, findings, or conclusions are those of the authors and do not necessarily reflect the views of the National Science Foundation, the University of Wisconsin–Madison, or Northern Illinois University.

for the three research questions raised in the study: (1) What is the impact of the MiC instructional approach on student achievement?; (2) How is the impact of instruction using MiC different from that of conventional instruction on student performance?; and (3) What variables associated with classroom instruction account for variation in student performance?

In the final chapter we summarize what we learned from the research and draw implications from the study for future curriculum summative evaluations in light of the pressures discussed in the initial chapter.

Acknowledgments

To carry out this study and produce the technical reports, monographs, and this book, we gratefully acknowledge the contributions of a host of others. First, we are grateful to the school personnel of the four research districts (administrators, mathematics coordinators, and, in particular, teachers) who were willing to participate, work our requests into their already filled schedules, and contribute information so we could investigate the use of new curricular materials. We also thank the two observers who provided extensive details about the lessons they observed for us. We are grateful that the publishers of *Mathematics in Context,* Encyclopædia Britannica, were willing to supply materials and provide consultants for our professional development work with study teachers. We appreciate the dedicated work of the research team and support staff at the Wisconsin Center for Education Research: graduate project assistants Jon Davis, Lesley R. Wagner, David C. Webb, Chul Lee, Supiya Balakul, and Joan Kwako; research assistants Theresa V. Arauco, Lorene Folgert, and Barbara Marten; external evaluator Norman Webb; administrative assistants including Fae Dremock, Mary Fish, Kay Schultz, and Kathleen Steele; and undergraduate project assistants who assisted in data entry. Each individually contributed to important aspects of the study and collectively made our job of summarizing the work easier. Finally, we are thankful for the significant contributions of Jan deLange and the staff of the Freudenthal Institute for the creation of the Problem Solving Assessment System, Ross Turner and Gail O'Connor of the Australian Council for Educational Research for their development of the Classroom Achievement Index, and Steven LeMire for his statistical advice and help.

Chapter 1

Summative evaluation of standards-based curricula

When new curricula are developed and published, the claims that they will improve student achievement are typically based on market research and/ or the claims of the authors as a consequence of one or more trials of the materials in classrooms. The validity of such claims for diverse sites is often questionable. What is needed is a summative evaluation of any particular curriculum. This involves large-scale studies that gather data to determine if the newly created product is ready for large-scale use. They are expensive and difficult to carry out. Unfortunately, examples of such studies are rare.[1]

In 1992 the National Science Foundation (NSF) funded several projects to develop new sets of instructional materials that reflected the reform vision of school mathematics espoused by the National Council of Teachers of Mathematics (NCTM, 1989). As the development of these materials was nearing completion, government agencies and educational researchers began to call for evidence that these were "research-based instructional materials" and could be used by other schools to improve student achievement.[2] Their intent was to ask the developers, or publishers, of such materials to go beyond the conventional "market research" toward more "scientific research"[3] to support any claims of increased student performance.

The National Research Council's review of the many studies related to the development of standards-based curricula found many reasonable design studies but no large-scale summative evaluations of any of the new curricula (National Research Council, 2004). The chapters in this book

---

1 The two large-scale evaluations involving mathematics texts in the U.S. since 1960 are the National Longitudinal Study of Mathematical Abilities conducted by the School Mathematics Study Group in the 1960s (Romberg & Wilson, 1972), and the IGE Evaluation Study conducted in the 1970s (Romberg, 1985).

2 For example, Feuer, Towne, & Shavelson, 2002; President's Committee of Advisors on Science and Technology-Panel on Educational Technology, 1997.

3 For example, Kilpatrick, Swaford, & Findell, 2001; Walker, 1992.

portray an example of a summative evaluation of a "standards-based" curriculum for middle schools, *Mathematics in Context*, and describe the complexity and difficulties of conducting such research. Furthermore, this study demonstrates the kinds of assessments that can be meaningfully done amidst the complexities of "real world" implementations.

To understand the pressures for well-conducted summative evaluations of the standards-based curricula, we have chosen to focus on:

1   summative evaluation as an aspect of curriculum research,
2   the fact that randomized experiments do not adequately address the contextual complexity of the instructional dynamics in classrooms, and
3   the potential of structural modeling as the basis for capturing the complexity of classroom instruction in such investigations.

Summative evaluation as an aspect of curriculum research

The evolution of research methods in education during the past quarter century has been discussed in several reports (e.g., Lagemann, 2000; Lagemann & Shulman, 1999; Shavelson & Towne, 2002), and specifically in mathematics education (e.g., Romberg, 1992; Schoenfeld, 1994, 2001). Researchers who have studied the development and use of new products, such as curricula, have used several different methods to gathering information and making judgments based on that data. For example, four general types of evaluations have been described in the literature: needs assessment, formative evaluation, summative evaluation, and illuminative evaluation (e.g., Romberg, 1992). All such evaluations involve gathering data to determine the usability of the product in educational settings, and as such should be considered as aspects of curriculum research.[4]

It should also be understood that federal-level insistence for information about the impact of new programs on student achievement is not new. Such calls began with the burst of reform programs associated with the mid-1960s Great Society initiatives in the United States. In areas as diverse as bilingual education, career education, compensatory programs, reading, or mathematics, little expertise in evaluation existed in the very agencies responsible for carrying out program evaluations. In fact, the initial training institute on program evaluation was held at the University of Illinois in 1963 under the direction of Lee Cronbach (Romberg, 1988).

> Clements (2007) argues that summative evaluations should use a broad set of instruments to assess the impact of the implementation

---

4 For a discussion of current thinking about curriculum research see Romberg, 2004a; Burkhardt, 2006; Clements, 2007.

on participating children, teachers, program administrators, and parents, as well as to document the fidelity of the implementation and the effects of the curriculum across diverse contexts . . . Ideally, because no set of experimental variables is complete or appropriate for each situation, qualitative inquiries [should] supplement these analyses.

(p. 53)

Thus, in summative evaluations the derived information comes from both quantitative and qualitative sources collected in several contexts to answer questions such as the following:

1   What is the impact of the use of the new program on student achievement?
2   How is the impact of instruction using the new curriculum different from that of conventional instruction on student performance?
3   What variables associated with classroom instruction account for variation in student performance?

The problem when attempting to answer such questions, as many authors have pointed out, is that schooling is a complex and dynamic social enterprise that does not fit the standard research methods prevalent in many other fields (Brown, 1992). In particular, the use of randomized experiments adapted from agricultural research simply cannot cope with the dynamics of classroom research.

Randomized experiments and the contextual complexity of classroom instruction

Driven by the spectacular success of experimental methods in agriculture and medicine, naïve policy makers have argued for the use of the "gold standard" of randomized controlled trials in summative evaluations of the new reform curricula so that "by harnessing the logical, conceptual, and computational power of mathematics and statistics, dubious notions about political and social dilemmas might be replaced with carefully reasoned and dispassionately tested scientific inferences" (DeNardo, 1998, p. 125). While the desire for reasoned empirically-based inferences is understandable, the belief that this can only be done via randomized experiments is not warranted.

The power of experimental methodology is based on three key assumptions:

1   treatment effects are additive,
2   treatment effects are constant, and

3   there is no interference between different experimental units (Cox, 1958).

If these assumptions are reasonable, then strong inferences are possible. Before explaining these assumptions and discussing their consequences, the three terms—treatments, effects, and experimental units—must be understood.[5]

Treatment. The objective of many agricultural experiments is to compare the yields of a number of plant varieties, fertilizers, or soil characteristics. The term "treatment", for example, might refer to the use of fertilizers. For curriculum studies, "treatment" would translate to use of a particular curriculum.

Effects. The term "effects" refers to yield or end product of a treatment. The number of "bushels of corn" in an agriculture study is an example of a yield. In curricular research this translates to assessment of performance at the termination of the "treatment". This is now most often accomplished by developing tests based on the goals of the instructional treatment.

Experimental unit. In agriculture the term "experimental unit" refers to the soil plots or "the smallest division of the experimental material such that any two units may receive different treatments in the actual experiment" (Cox, 1958, p. 2). In curricular summative evaluations, the "experimental unit" should be the students and teachers in a classroom or school using the new curricula.

Treatment effects are additive

The mathematics of determining experimental effects is based on Equation 1 (Cox, 1958, p. 14). Equation 1 says that the total quantitative effect of yield (y) after a

$$y = u + t \tag{1}$$

treatment can be broken down into two sub-quantities: u—a quantity depending only on the particular experimental unit, and t—a quantity depending only on the treatment used. There are *two immediate consequences* of this assumption. The first is the quantifiability of the first three terms—y, u, and t. While it is true that one mark of a mature science is the possession of sophisticated measurement instruments and techniques, we must admit that at present in education, we are not able to quantify with any validity or accuracy many terms in an educational setting. The

---

5 For a more complete discussion of the assumptions underlying randomized experiments see Romberg, 2004a.

second consequence of the additive assumption allows the possibility for adding or subtracting these treatment effects in an algebraic manner in order to remove the quantity depending upon the experimental unit. For example, one can estimate differences between two treatment effects. If measurements are taken after two different treatments, they can be subtracted. The following set of equations shows this algebraic process.

$$y_1 = u + t_1 \qquad \text{(Measurement after Treatment 1)} \qquad (2)$$

$$y_2 = u + t_2 \qquad \text{(Measurement after Treatment 2)} \qquad (3)$$

$$y_1 - y_2 = t_1 - t_2 \qquad\qquad\qquad\qquad\qquad\qquad\qquad\qquad (4)$$

Equation 4 says that the difference between the final measurements after Treatments 1 and 2 ($y_1 - y_2$) can be considered to also be the difference between the two effects due only to Treatments 1 and 2 ($t_1 - t_2$). Note, however, that this equation is correct only if the effects depending on the unit (the us) are equal for different units. These conditions are assumed to be true when there is no systematic bias, which differentiates the experimental units. *Control of bias* is accomplished by random assignment of experimental units to the alternate treatments.

In fact, it is this alternate treatment randomized experimental design for classroom research that many policy makers are calling for when one does summative evaluations of the standards-based curricula. One treatment involves an experimental treatment based on the new curricula, the other treatment being whatever had been typically done (the conventional treatment), and the comparison is made in terms of differences between treatment groups on some post-test. Unfortunately, comparable classrooms assigned randomly to alternate treatments often is not feasible for a variety of reasons—some of them ethical. Hence any claim of important differences of yield between treatments is logically suspect.

If random assignment is not possible, quasi-experiments are sometimes appropriate. This involves "matching" experimental units on some characteristics, and adjusting achievement scores to account for some of those differences. However, as Campbell and Stanley (1963) so forcefully point out, there are several sources of potential invalidity to this strategy such as history, maturation, instrumentation, test treatment interaction, and so forth. Investigators of classrooms simply cannot blindly use differences in scores as estimates of treatment effects.

Constancy of treatment effects

In an attempt to increase the generalizability of the findings, most researchers replicate the instructional procedure by using the basic program in two or more settings. This assumption says that treatment effect does not change when the treatment is given to two different units. Algebraically, this assumption allows Equation 5 to represent the measured effect after a specific treatment on one unit (u_1), and Equation 6 to represent the measured effect of the same treatment upon a different unit.

$$y_1 = u_1 + t \tag{5}$$

$$y_2 = u_2 + t \tag{6}$$

Since treatment effect is assumed to be the same for these two different units (e.g., the same fertilizer is used with both units), the subtraction of Equation 6 from Equation 5 states a very important consequence of this assumption (see Equation 7).

$$y_1 - y_2 = u_1 - u_2 \tag{7}$$

Equation 7 states that if two different experimental units (u_1 and u_2) receive the same treatment, then the differences in effect (y_1 and y_2) are only due to differences in units. With this assumption, when one compares the end of treatment measures, one is also comparing the differences between the experimental units. Note, following this argument, if u_1 and u_2 were identical units, the difference in treatment effects should be zero. However, if aspects of instruction procedures are adapted for different classes using the same curriculum, one would actually anticipate different treatment effects. In fact, the difference between instruction in one classroom and instruction in another class is likely to vary considerably. Such differences are both natural and beneficial. Instructional events are not mechanistic routines to be blindly followed. Real events grow, change, and develop as the human beings involved in the event interact. In fact, it is the actual patterns of interactions, rather than the intended treatments, that are the important features of classroom instruction for policy makers, teachers, and other researchers.

Lack of interference of experimental units

This assumption says that when more than one experimental unit is used, there is no interference or interaction between the units. This assumption is particularly important if statistical analysis is to be made of the observations since the statistics are based on an assumption of independence of observations (or unit measurements). If the experimental units really were independent classes in different schools, then one might argue lack of interference between the classes. This assumption is problematic when one uses individual students as the experimental unit. As students are exposed to new material, we expect them to assimilate those new ideas into their own personal meanings or ideational scaffolding. We *expect* the same instructional event to have different effects on different students. Some will assimilate and use lots of new information in one way, others may generate quite different kinds of new information and relationships. Researchers now have generally agreed that unless the influence of individual difference variables is considered, predicted outcomes of instructional events will be masked by within-treatment variation. Persons indeed do differ in how they respond to the same information or the same instructional procedures. Thus, the assumption that treatment effects are constant is simply false in most classroom circumstances.

Also, such interference between units is the essential interaction between human beings one expects in classes. In fact, investigators have typically assumed that the treatment effect for a class is simply an aggregate of individual effects (individual students considered as the experimental units). The argument is usually that "we teach pupils, not classes". This simply is not the reality of dynamic classroom instruction. By assuming no interaction, the researcher closes his eyes to the essence of the event.

In summary, use of randomized experiments for summative evaluations is rarely warranted because typically all three of its assumptions are violated. Classroom instruction occurs in the context of schools where it is frequently impossible to randomly assign schools or classrooms to alternate curricula, where variation in use of the curricula is expected, and where students are expected to interact during classroom instruction.

Also, it should be noted that when one then adds (1) the small number of classes in suburban schools, (2) the common use of student as the unit of investigation, (3) the often poor documentation of actual differences in treatments as implemented in classrooms, and (4) the frequent use of poor or invalid outcome measures, it is no wonder that such comparative research is often seen as problematic.

Structural modeling of classroom instruction

If randomized experiments are inappropriate, what scientific methodology is appropriate? Stewart, Cartier, & Passmore (2001) point out that too often research methods have focused on "a narrowly circumscribed, experimental, perspective on the intellectual activities of scientists" (p. 2). They go on to argue that:

> Many sciences do not extensively utilize true experiments (the methods of which are idealized in traditional science textbooks) as they conduct empirical inquiries. . . . Conceptual problems require that scientists confront the coherence of their "explanations" by examining the internal coherence of explanatory models as well as their

relationship to other models, methodological norms, and predominant worldviews of the culture in which science is practiced. It is indeed unfortunate that science is generally portrayed to students as strictly empirical, with little attention given to the deep conceptual issues that have legitimately occupied scientists both past and present.

(pp. 4–5)

In fact, reliable and reasoned inferences are more likely from studies that address conceptual issues within an emerging framework, than via comparative experiments. It should be understood that the development of such frameworks is in fact what scientific inquiry is about. It is our contention that using a structural model of classroom instruction is an appropriate methodology for conducting summative evaluations of standards-based curricula.

To build such a model about instruction we recognize that a classroom includes a group of students, a teacher, and the social expectations that, as a consequence of instruction over some period of time, the students will learn with understanding specific important aspects of mathematics. Building a model involves specifying the assumptions, concepts, and principles one believes are operating in the real situation. Such specification must, of course, be selective in its bias. For the example in this book, we began the process by using four characteristics described by Popkewitz, Tabachnick, & Wehlage (1982) to highlight the problematic features of classroom instruction.

1 Schools are goal directed. Schools for all children are historically recent and were created to transmit aspects of the culture to the young and to direct students toward and provide them an opportunity for self-fulfillment.
2 Schools are places where conceptions of knowledge are distributed and maintained. One important decision that must be made by those who organize schools is to select what to teach. This decision must grow out of a consensus on what it is important for the young to know.
3 Schools are places of work, where students, teachers, and administrators act to alter and improve their world; produce positive social relations; and realize specific human purposes. For example, it is assumed that knowledge will be acquired by the young via some deliberately created activities organized and managed by the teacher.
4 The work in schools is carried out by using an established technology.

The reform vision of school mathematics focuses on changing how the work of teachers and in turn the work of students is carried out when a school has chosen to use a standards-based curriculum.

The materials evaluated in this study, *Mathematics in Context* (MiC), differ from most conventional mathematics texts in both content and expected pedagogy. The content of MiC includes more than just the focus on arithmetic skills found in conventional materials. Instead, the content in MiC emphasizes making connections among mathematical topics and domains and making connections between mathematics and real-world problem solving. Its roots are grounded in quantitative and spatial situations, and referred to in MiC as strands, are *number* (whole numbers, common fractions, ratio, decimal fractions, percents, and integers), *algebra* (creation of expressions, tables, graphs, and formulas from patterns and functions), *geometry* (measurement, spatial visualization, synthetic geometry, coordinate and transformational geometry), and *statistics and probability* (data visualization, chance, distribution and variability, and quantification of expectations).

The intended pedagogy is different from the conventional formal presentation of material parceled into two-page unchanging spreads with emphasis on review of previous material and quiet independent seatwork. By contrast, in MiC the teacher selects and modifies tasks in the instructional unit that involve important mathematics, allow for student discussion, and include both independent and collaborative investigation of complex, non-routine problems. Students are expected to explore mathematical relationships, develop their own strategies for solving problems, use appropriate problem-solving tools, work together cooperatively, and value each other's strategies. They are encouraged to explain their thinking as well as their solutions. The teacher's role in the instructional process involves capitalizing on students' reasoning and continually introducing and negotiating with students the emergence of shared terms, symbols, rules, and strategies, with an eye to encouraging students to reflect on what they learn.

With this perspective, a simplification or idealization is a crucial stage, since the general problem of describing the work of both teachers and students when teaching this curriculum is exceedingly complex and involves many processes. The model itself contains a list of variables, and a list of relationships specifying the links that are hypothesized to exist between variables. The real power of structural modeling lies both in the representation process (because it forces one to consider the relationship between variables), and in what one can do with those representations. The statements about relationships can be viewed as a set of premises from which other sets of consequences can be deduced (predictions can be made). Finally, if each of the variables in the model can be reliably scaled, then the linkages, or paths between variables, can be statistically determined.[6]

---

6 See Asher, 1976; Hayduk, 1987; or Heise, 1978 for examples of how this is done.

When building such a model one should recognize that a model is not a completely accurate representation of a real situation; it is only an attempt to capture some key components and their interrelationships with respect to classroom instruction. The utility and status of a model depends on social agreement and the empirical evidence that validates the model. Real situations, such as mathematics instruction in classrooms, are rarely well defined and are often embedded in an environment that makes a clear statement of the situation hard to obtain.

In summary, building a structural model together with the development of composite scales based on the variables in such a model we are confident is an effective way to carry out classroom research in school settings.

The structural model we used in this study (Romberg & Shafer, 2005) is composed of variables and their theoretical interrelationships (represented by arrows in the model). This model, illustrated in Figure 1.1, includes 14 variables in five categories (prior, independent, intervening, outcome, and consequent).[7]

Prior variables permit one to take into account conditions at the start of the study that are likely to affect instruction as data are gathered over time. This structural model takes into account three variables: background and prior knowledge of students, teacher background, and the social context or culture in which particular schools operate.

Independent variables represented in the structural model include curricular content and materials, the support environment available for students and teachers, teacher knowledge, and teacher professional responsibility.

Intervening variables are directly influenced by the independent variables and significantly affect student outcomes. The intervening variables capture an array of complex teacher decisions in planning and interactive decision-making. These decisions also influence the type of assessment information gathered about each student's knowledge and dispositions. Intervening variables also capture students' active involvement in learning and applying their knowledge as part of everyday classroom events. In the structural model, three intervening variables are identified: pedagogical decisions, classroom events, and student pursuits.

Outcome and consequent variables of instruction are that students will acquire knowledge of concepts in various domains and proficiency with skills, and the ability to apply their knowledge in various situations, in addition to developing favorable attitudes. The three outcome variables we include in the structural model are knowledge, application, and attitudes. The consequent variable refers to students' further education, employment, etc. In this case it refers to transition into high school and the number and type of courses which students take in high school.

---

7 This research model is a revised version of the original in Romberg (1987).

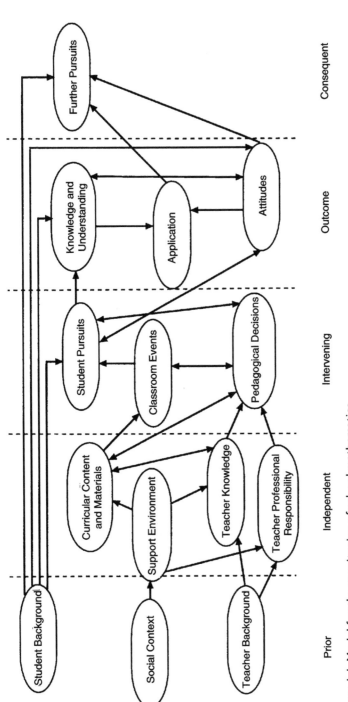

Figure 1.1 Model for the monitoring of school mathematics.

This model provided us with the basis for gathering and interpreting information about mathematics instruction and changes in school mathematics being initiated by the use of MiC curriculum materials. It demonstrates the belief that mathematics teaching is complex and that changes cannot be simplistically studied.

Then, if we could develop appropriate indices to scale the variability associated with each variable, useful information should be available for policy makers, school personnel, and researchers. It should be made clear that the structural model, as illustrated, is a static model. It can only be used to investigate the relationships between variables at a particular point in time, with a sample from particular populations. Furthermore, the unit of analysis must be class (or school), and the scaled links between variables refer to "averages" or "tendencies", since exceptions are to be expected.

Indices

To use the structural model shown in Figure 1.1 for analytic purposes, one or more indices (scales) must be created for each variable. The purpose of each index would be to capture the variability across classes (or schools) with respect to the variable. For example, to measure content, several indices (such as an index of content relevance, an index of content coverage, and an index of correspondence with assessment of knowledge) could be developed. Content relevance includes balance between the learning of concepts, skills, and applications; emphasis given to specific topics; adherence to the logic of the discipline; incorporation of research-based knowledge about learning and teaching; and relationship to proposed content changes. Such an index would be an important development, since the current practice of accepting similar text titles as representing exposure to similar material is totally inadequate. Another example could involve using teacher logs to determine which aspects of the available curriculum are actually taught and emphasized. Another index should be created to assess the degree of correspondence between the instructional content of a text and the assessment tasks used to measure knowledge. A major task we faced in conducting the study was the development and validation of indices for the variables in the model.

Indicators

As described, an index is only a measure of a variable. As a thermometer only gives a measure of body temperature, a comparison of that measure with a standard (e.g., 98.6°F for normal body temperature), a prior measure, or a different measure, is needed to determine health. Indicators are new indices created from a prior index by making such ratios or comparisons. Comprehensive examination of such variables involves both qualitative and quantitative methods that explicate potential differences in student performance as a consequence of different treatments.

Because collinearity across indices posed a serious interpretation problem, a simplified model was designed during 1998–1999 when Professor Romberg was a Fellow at the Center for Advanced Study in the Behavioral Sciences at Stanford. The statistics working group at the Center, headed by Lincoln Moses, examined the indices and the analysis plan for the study and suggested that four composite variables, or indicators, be created. This later became five composite variables during the examination of the information gathered in the study. The simplified model describes the relationship between variations in classroom achievement (CA), aggregated by strand, or total performance can be attributed to variations in opportunity to learn with understanding (OTLu), preceding achievement (PA), method of instruction (I), and school capacity (SC). This relationship can be expressed as—

$$CA = OTLu + PA + I + SC$$

These composite indicators, based on one or more indices created for each variable in the original model, were then to be created. The indices were intended to capture the variability across classes (and schools) in relation to each variable in the structural model. In summary, what the naïve person may view as a simple comparative experiment, turns out to be very complex when examining differences between instruction in different social contexts with considerable variation in prior, independent, intervening, outcome, and consequent variables. This happens because of the difficulty involved in arranging student and school settings to control potential sources of possible co-variation, a control more easily achieved in laboratory settings. The dynamic interplay of all these variables has an impact on student learning, and as such, these variables must be considered in any comparison of instructional programs in real classrooms.

Conclusion

The primary role of researchers is to provide our society with reliable evidence to back up claims. Research that focuses on providing such knowledge about classroom instruction is critical. By gathering evidence and constructing reasonable arguments, researchers substantiate conjectures. This process is arduous and endless. Findings, once achieved, do not stay "finished" and complete: The evidential base—what constitutes a reasonable argument and the given purposes—continually changes. Regardless of such changes in context, however, research is valued as a way of demonstrating *reliable* knowledge. By conducting summative evaluations using structural models one is able to produce reasonable evidence that contributes to understanding the impact of using a standards-based curriculum on student mathematics achievement.

In Chapters 2 through 10 we have attempted to summarize the steps taken in carrying out a large-scale summative evaluation of *Mathematics in Context*. In so doing we have tried to include the frustrations, problems, and limits of our efforts as well as the successes. Any reader interested in conducting such a study will find that one's dreams of what can be accomplished are unlikely to be met. The variety of school contexts, coupled with the complexity of classroom interactions and limits to what information can be collected, make the findings an incomplete shadow of the dreams. Nevertheless, we learned a lot about the process of implementing a standards-based program and how to conduct summative evaluations. In Chapter 11 we summarize what we learned and reflect on the process of carrying out such studies.

Chapter 2

Proposing to study standards-based curriculum implementation

We want children to be problem solvers, inference makers, thinkers, and doers, and be able to access knowledge as we move into the new century, as we go into a technological age . . .

Assistant Principal, District 4

We've had a real problem in the district's history of having students who have memorized things and didn't really have any understanding of how to use them.

Principal, District 3

I think performance is probably the key word: What can students do with the skills and the knowledge that they have? How do they apply that to solve problems?

Principal, District 1

In 1995, we submitted a proposal to NSF to document the impact of *Mathematics in Context* (MiC) on the mathematical performance of students; to compare their performance with that of students who have been studying using conventional materials; and to examine district, school, teacher, and pedagogical differences associated with variation in student performance in the use of a standards-based curriculum. (See Romberg [2004c] and Romberg & Shafer [2004b] for more details.)

MiC is one of the several projects funded by NSF to develop new sets of instructional materials that reflected the reform vision of school mathematics espoused by the National Council of Teachers of Mathematics (NCTM, 1989). The approach was to design instructional activities that focus on changing how the work of teachers and in turn the work of students involved selecting contexts that could be mathematized, an approach that was used in reforming Dutch school mathematics curriculum, termed Realistic Mathematics Education. This instructional approach is based on the ideas of the mathematician Hans Freudenthal (1983), who believed that "students are entitled to recapitulate in a fashion the learning process of mankind" (p. ix). He stated that "mathematical structures are not presented to the learner so that they might be filled with realities … They arise, instead, from reality itself, which is not a fixed datum, but expands continuously in individual and collective learning process" (Freudenthal, 1987, p. 280). The sequencing of activities requires making fundamental decisions about the intended pathways toward developing students' mathematical understanding. In these sequences, the initial contexts function as paradigm cases, the instruction includes activities that lead to students' modeling of their informal mathematics using simple notations, and students' models, with appropriate guidance from teachers, evolve into models for increasingly abstract mathematical reasoning.

The MiC materials consist of 40 curriculum units (10 at each grade level 5–8), a teacher's guide for each unit, including assessment materials, and two sets of supplementary materials, *News in Numbers* and *Number Tools*. As described in Chapter 1, the materials differ from most conventional mathematics texts in both content and expected pedagogy.

Adapting research practices to the "laboratory"

In designing the study, we wanted to provide a response to the many calls for evidence showing that a new standards-based curriculum has an impact on student achievement, but we also wanted to find a way of documenting the considerable variation in teacher implementation of any curriculum and provide evidence of the impact of (and lack of) treatment fidelity. During both the pilot- and field-tests of the MiC materials, information was gathered from teachers, students, administrators, and parents through surveys, teacher logs, unit tests, and classroom observations. Most of the data were used to revise and improve the activities and the teacher guides that accompany the units. However, in field-testing MiC, we had observed frequent material substitution and supplementation with conventional materials, familiar (and therefore comfortable) pedagogical practices that went counter to the intent of the curriculum, and teacher lack of familiarity with mathematical content, among other behaviors—all of which affected student opportunity to learn comprehensive mathematics content in depth and with understanding (Romberg, 1997).

We note that these variations in classroom instruction were observed in the practices of teachers committed to reform, who taught in predominantly suburban schools, who wanted to "do a good job" of curriculum implementation—and who often did not recognize the mismatch in their classroom practices. The dynamic interplay of such classroom variations has an impact on the effectiveness of any reform curriculum as well as on student learning and achievement. Although the results on measures of achievement that confirm improved student mathematical performance are very important, we contend that relying solely on outcome measures to judge the value of a standards-based program is insufficient.

In response to what we had seen in classrooms taught by reform teachers, we also wanted to compare instruction using MiC with conventional instruction to demonstrate a practical method of gathering and documenting valid evidence that took into account the classroom and teacher differences. To gather such evidence, a four-year combined longitudinal/cross-sectional comparative study was proposed. In that proposal three questions were raised.

1   What is the impact of the MiC instructional approach on student performance?

MiC is a four-year program designed for Grades 5–8, and its design included the deliberate structuring of activities so that over the four years students progressed from informal to formal ideas in four content strands. Thus, a longitudinal study designed to track student overall mathematical growth and growth in each of the content stands was warranted.

2   How is this impact different from that of traditional instruction on student performance?

To answer this question we proposed to gather similar data for students in matched conventional mathematics classes as was to be gathered for students using MiC materials.

3   What variables associated with classroom instruction account for variation in student performance?

This question was raised for three reasons. First, although the results on measures of achievement that confirm improved student mathematical performance are very important, we contend that just relying on outcome measures to judge the value of a standards-based program is insufficient. Second, in the field-testing of the materials there was considerable variation in the observed patterns of instruction. Thus, it is not enough to consider outcomes in the absence of the effects of the instructional setting in which student learning is situated and the students' opportunity to learn comprehensive mathematics content in depth and with understanding. The dynamic interplay of such variables has an impact on student learning. Third, because during the field-testing of the program this observed variation occurred with teachers committed to reform in predominantly suburban schools, we were anxious to see how the program would be used during initial implementation in urban, high poverty, school districts with minority students and, in turn, what the impact of its use would be on student performance.

Given these questions and concerns, the research design for the study had two primary components. First, to answer Questions 1 and

3 we proposed to use a structural research model to examine the impact of the multivariate classroom interventions anticipated when teachers use MiC materials in their classrooms. Structural modeling involves identifying the key variables hypothesized to be critical and locating causal paths between the variables. Methodological issues that arise involve attempts to capture, interpret, and report variation in the methods used to support curricular change, implementation of reform-based curricula, and student performance. Technically, this involves specification, measurement, estimation, and statistical inference, rather than the control of sources of variations. Comprehensive examination of such variables involves both qualitative and quantitative methods that explicate differences in student performance as a consequence of studying either reform-based or conventional curricula. As described in Chapter 1, this process of structural modeling together with the development of composite scales based on such a model we contend is an effective way to carry out curricular research in school settings.

To answer Question 2 we proposed to supplement the structural model with a quasi-experiment by comparing student performance in a sample of classrooms using the MiC materials with that in a similar sample of classrooms using traditional materials. The assignment of students to classrooms was nonrandom, and comparable information was collected on the variables in the structural model for both groups. This design allowed us to build a case as to whether observed group differences on outcome measures were a consequence of using a particular curriculum or were an inherent product of preexisting group differences described through some of the variables in the research model (Campbell & Stanley, 1963).

This process of structural modeling, together with the development of model-based composite scales, has proven to be an effective way to carry out research in school settings and should be of interest to educational researchers and potential funding agencies. However, as we looked at causal paths, we found ourselves redefining the primary unit of analysis, realizing that the root force of implementation grew out of the classroom, not the district or even the school.

Again, as discussed in Chapter 1, we note that there is a long-held belief that randomized comparative experiments provide the best evidence for making causal statements about alternate education practices. Unfortunately, examining the achievement effects of instructional and curricular differences in the social laboratory of a school, with little real possibility of "controlled" variation and yet substantial dynamic impact on student achievement, is "messy" and complex. This does not mean quality research cannot be done, but rather indicates the difficulty involved

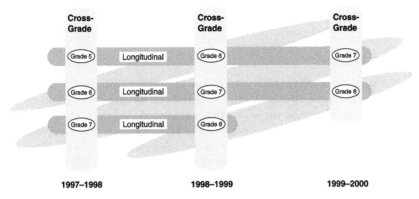

Figure 2.1 Structure of the proposed studies.

in arranging student and school settings to control potential sources of variation. As in other social sciences, researchers can build formal models identifying the key variables and locate causal paths between those variables.

In the proposal, the data we planned to use to answer the three questions was to be based on 17 separate studies: eight grade-level-by-year studies, six cross-sectional studies, and three longitudinal studies (see Figure 2.1). Thus, the title of the proposed study was "The Longitudinal/ Cross-Sectional Study of the Impact of Teaching Mathematics using *Mathematics in Context* on Student Achievement".

Scaling up research design to agency requirements

Several changes in what we originally proposed were made as a result of negotiations with NSF. We simplified instrumentation plans and changed the time line to accommodate (in the first year of the grant) the development, tailoring, and field-testing of 22 instruments, including specific protocols for observations and interviews, questionnaires and teaching logs, and a targeted student attitude inventory (Shafer, 2004b). In that first year, we also developed the assessments for student performance and designed a relational, modular, and, thus, highly extensible database that would accommodate a diverse group of users with varying database skills and could house the enormity of data we proposed to collect on participating students, schools, teachers, district, administrators, and classrooms.

The final operational plan of the study also included the development and implementation of professional development institutes for study teachers and principals, continuous data collection, ongoing development and revision of study assessments, database modifications, and coding and analysis strategies.

Summary

Our initial proposal to NSF involved a rational, idealized portrayal of how one could examine in depth the details of the implementation of a standards-based middle school curriculum in urban schools. Information from field-tests during development of the MiC materials raised questions about the variations in what teachers did in their classrooms. In particular, would variations in implementation of the MiC materials affect student performance in various school settings and how would that student performance differ from that of comparable students in conventional classrooms? The proposed structural model along with a quasi-experimental design to be carried out in a number of schools would provide important information for school personnel as well as researchers.

In retrospect, our vision was overly ambitious. To carry out the proposed study would require considerably more resources than NSF was willing to allocate and more staff and personnel than we could have to work on the project. Nevertheless, in 1996 NSF decided to fund the project following considerable negotiations on details of the study.

Chapter 3

Setting the foundation: initiation of the study

> We initially planned to involve six districts, with two-thirds of the study teachers and students in each district using MiC, and the remaining teachers and students using the conventional textbooks already in place in the schools
>
> (Shafer, 2004b)

Site selection process

The process of finding research sites began in the fall 1996, and selection was based on several criteria. First, because NSF requested that participating districts already be involved in systemic initiatives for reforming mathematics education, we began by contacting districts involved in Urban Systemic Initiatives (USI) or State Systemic Initiatives (SSI), university faculty who participated in mathematics education reform efforts across the United States, and school districts that had participated in the pilot- and field-test phases of the development of MiC. Four systemic initiatives, five university faculty, and eight pilot- and field-test sites were contacted, and negotiations were actively pursued with nine school districts.

The second set of selection criteria was related to research conditions. Consideration was given to the size, location (rural, suburban, urban), and demographics of potential districts; the number of mathematics classes taught by fifth-grade and middle-school teachers; the typical class size and length of class periods; student mobility; and availability of mathematics books for student use.

The third set of criteria was related to teacher experience with MiC prior to the study. Specifically, we sought urban districts serving students from low-income families in which teachers had been exposed to MiC or had taught pilot- or field-test units. In one interested district that committed to using one MiC unit before the end of the 1996–1997 school year, we conducted a workshop focused on implementation issues such as teaching MiC in block schedules, integration of MiC units into established problem-solving classes, and parent involvement sessions.

The last set of criteria, and the first major complicating issue we encountered, was related to the nature of a comparative study. Principals of schools involved in systemic initiatives did not want to be perceived as disregarding efforts to reform mathematics curriculum and instruction, and neither district administrators nor principals wanted to appear to be withholding from students the opportunity of learning mathematics in more powerful ways. In light of these concerns, we modified the research design to allow exclusion of the comparative element in two districts. In this modified design, MiC would be the only curriculum used by teachers and students, and classroom interaction data would not be collected.

A second complicating issue related to the feeder patterns of elementary schools emerged as we were selecting middle schools. In some cases, districts were unable to identify feeder patterns in which administrators of the affected elementary and middle schools were interested in participating in the study. Middle schools also typically received incoming students from many elementary schools, making it difficult to keep students together in classes of participating teachers for all years of a longitudinal study. (This actually proved impossible, despite earlier district and principal assurances that this could be done.)

In March 1997, meetings were held with key district administrative personnel in each of the interested districts to discuss (among other items) the evidence of student achievement from MiC field-test sites, the nature and importance of a longitudinal study, participation details, terms of the subcontract, teacher compensation for participation, the possible benefits to the students, the recent state-mandated Grade 8 district algebra initiatives, and "best" ways to approach parents. Two districts were identified as strong candidates for the comparative study, and contracts were negotiated.

In May 1997, a meeting was held in Madison for district site coordinators and on-site observers. Also attending were representatives from three interested, but still uncommitted school districts. The purpose of the meeting was to provide opportunities for personnel in selected and potential districts to meet and to provide suggestions for final forms of study instruments.

By the fall of 1997, four school districts had committed to the research. Districts 1 and 2 would participate in the comparative study. In these districts, data were gathered on all research variables, which included data from classroom observations and daily teaching logs. District 1, located in an eastern urban region, had a student population of 30% African–American students, 12% Hispanic students, and 58% White students. About one-third of the students in this district were eligible for government-funded lunch programs. District 2, located in a large southeastern urban area, had a student population of 33% African–American students, 52% Hispanic students, and 15% White students. Over 50% of the students in the district were eligible for government-funded lunch programs. Districts 3 and 4 would participate in the modified research design. Classroom observation and teacher log data were not gathered in these districts. District 3, located in a western working-class suburban area, contained only four schools, each specializing in three or four grade levels. The student population was predominantly White students. About 10–20% of the students were eligible for government-funded lunch programs. District 4, located in a large eastern urban area, included students from one middle school, which had a student population of 50% African–American students, 37% Hispanic students, and 13% White students and Other students.[1] Over 50% of the students were eligible for government-funded lunch programs. (District 4 would have no fifth-grade cohort.)

District administrators and on-site coordinators (selected by the districts) were asked to select schools that were representative of the district population, rather than selecting schools with extremely low- or high-achieving student populations. Principals of the selected schools chose the study teachers. Teachers, in turn, were asked to select classes of students with average mathematical abilities rather than classes of low ability or classes in honors programs.

With the implementation of the modified study design, the number of participating teachers using MiC grew as a percentage of total participants, and the opportunities to compare curriculum effect diminished accordingly. Nonetheless, although the modified design constrained our attempts at comparison, the change proved a fertile opportunity for a broader and deeper examination of the elements of teacher community, beliefs, and instructional practices that created the class culture and norms that can make implementation of a reform curriculum successful in enhancing student learning and achievement.

Operationalization

During the year prior to data collection, 22 instruments were designed to address the 14 variables in the research model. District and school profiles, teacher and student questionnaires, the teaching log, the classroom observation instrument, and the Student Attitude Inventory were based on instruments from prior studies of systemic change in school districts, content taught in mathematics and science classes, and student dispositions toward mathematics. These instruments were revised based on

---

1 The category for Other students includes Asian students, Native American students, Multiracial students, and other students.

pilot-testing with both MiC field-test students and students who studied conventional curricula. Input from district site coordinators, observers, and principals was also considered during a meeting in Madison in May 1997. Information about the outcome measures developed for the study is found in Chapter 6.

A retired mathematics teacher in each district was selected with district input to conduct classroom observations and principal and teacher interviews. The observers worked with graduate project assistants to ensure interrater reliability in non-study classrooms in Madison, with videotaped lessons, and in study classrooms (Shafer, Wagner, & Davis, 1997a). Discussions between observers and project assistants centered on consistency of ratings and the written evidence that supported the ratings.

Data collection began in the summer of 1997. Throughout the summer, lists of schools and teachers were finalized by participating districts. Teacher consent forms were mailed with information about the study, teacher compensation, and teacher responsibilities in the study. School districts were also asked to send the standardized test scores for study classes. The first professional development institutes for teachers were held, and teachers completed consent forms and initial questionnaires. In the fall of 1997, parental consent for student participation was obtained, principals and teachers were interviewed about their views of teaching and learning mathematics and the school context, classroom observations began, and initial teacher logs were sent to the research center. Students completed the Student Questionnaire, the Student Attitude Inventory, and the *Collis-Romberg Mathematical Problem Solving Profiles* (Form A; Collis & Romberg, 1992). District administrators and principals completed District and School Profiles. In the spring of 1998, teachers were interviewed about instructional planning and classroom interaction, and they completed two questionnaires. Students completed the Student Attitude Inventory and the two grade-specific assessments designed for the study. In 1998–1999 and 1999–2000, data collection followed a similar plan. Students who were new to the study completed the initial student instruments, and in the final spring of each student's participation, the *Collis-Romberg Mathematical Problem Solving Profiles* (Form B) were administered. In attempts to follow study students into Grade 9, a questionnaire was sent to each student via his/her high school counselor. After a low response rate the first time, this questionnaire was not distributed in subsequent years.

As part of the project's ongoing work with study teachers, two types of professional development were provided. First, four-day on-site summer institutes were held in Districts 1 and 2 during August each year. Another professional development opportunity was for teachers to learn about and score portions of the Problem Solving Assessments. More detailed information about the professional development provided by the study is found in the next chapter.

Unanticipated constraints

Although the operational plan was clearly set out in district contracts and in day-to-day operations, changes to the plan occurred (Shafer, 2004a). In part, these changes grew out of the complex set of personalities, institutional policies, and cultures of individual schools. We also note, however, that some changes grew out of the striking attrition affecting both MiC and non-MiC cohorts (both students and teachers), which proved more of a constraint to treatment comparison than did the limitations imposed by the study design. This attrition made comparative inferences in the later years of the study highly problematic. In 1997–1998, for example, there were 579 sixth-grade students in the study (422 MiC students). In 1999–2000, this now eighth-grade group included only 303 students (248 MiC students). Initially, we had intended to study more or less intact groups of students over the three years of the study, but this proved impractical in three of the four districts. For example, 90% of the students in District 1, 96% of the students in District 2, and 43% of the students in District 3 who completed both study assessments in Grade 5 did not remain in the study throughout all three years.

Similar attrition was found for teachers. Many teachers (37% of the sixth-grade teachers, 41% of the seventh-grade teachers, and 31% of the eighth-grade teachers) left the study prematurely. Teachers moved to non-study schools, went on family leave, were reassigned to another grade level, accepted administrative positions, or resigned from the study. In most cases, additional teachers (15% of the sixth-grade study teachers, 31% of the seventh-grade teachers, and 23% of the eighth-grade teachers) were asked to join the study. Also, although we anticipated changes in personnel, we did not expect that teachers might move from one grade level to the next with their classes (11% of the sixth-grade teachers and 14% of the seventh-grade teachers) and, therefore, needed to prepare for teaching different units every year.

Summary

Our work with school districts was both challenging and rewarding. We feel that our extensive attempts to collect quality data were successful in many ways. We were able to collect rich classroom observation data, record teacher accounts of what transpired in study classes, and gather assessment data for many students longitudinally. In the finish, teachers appreciated our continuing efforts to support their teaching of comprehensive mathematics content to diverse student groups. District and school personnel requested and received support from the research team to present information about MiC and about the study at teachers' meetings and meetings of parent or community organizations. These gestures of goodwill and support enhanced the extensive data collection process.

Chapter 4

Building a culture of support for reform: implementation of professional development

The project staff provided two types of professional development activities, open to all mathematics staff in each district, as part of our ongoing work with teachers and principals: summer institutes and scoring institutes (Shafer, 2004a). During summer institutes participants learned about the study and engaged in discussions of reform in mathematics curriculum, instruction, and assessment. The scoring institutes were held each spring for participants to learn about the Problem Solving Assessments designed for the study, review actual student responses from their district, and score portions of the assessments.

Summer institutes

Four-day institutes were held in August in Districts 1 and 2 each study year. These institutes allowed the research team to establish rapport with teachers and district personnel, but they also provided occasions for the research team to explain details about the study and for teachers to review all study instruments. The institutes also served as incentives for districts and support for study teachers.

During the summer institutes in 1997, the first day was devoted to information about the study goals, research design, and study instruments. On the remaining days, concurrent workshops were held for teachers who used conventional curricula and for MiC teachers. Institutes for teachers who used conventional curricula focused on alignment of curriculum, instruction, and assessment. The institutes began with a discussion of why the NCTM *Standards* (NCTM, 1989, 1991, 1995) were developed, the importance of all students developing mathematical power, and two working assumptions about the changes envisioned in the *Standards*—that teachers are the key figures in changing the ways in which mathematics is taught and learned in schools, and that these changes require that teachers have the long-term support and adequate resources necessary to promote professional growth. The alignment of curriculum, instruction, and assessment was presented through a discussion of the effects of the state mathematics framework on both the content they taught and their instruction. Another focus of these institutes was classroom assessment practice. Teachers viewed two videos of classroom interaction, and they discussed opportunities for students to prepare and react to mathematical arguments, classroom interaction that attends to individual needs, and the importance of lesson summaries. Teachers also talked about ways to generate meaningful class discussions and procedural versus conceptual understanding. In the remaining portion of the institutes, teachers learned about assessment of student understanding through non-routine tasks; intersections among scoring, feedback, grading, and reflection on teaching; and the possibilities for assessment through the use of multiple-day and long-term assessment projects.

For MiC teachers, the research team selected major themes or substrands across units as the focus of the activities for each content strand. Teachers worked through student lessons in cooperative groups, learned about methods for generating classroom discussions, and talked about linkages among the lessons. The philosophy of MiC was illustrated with the algebra strand, and work in the number strand focused on developing rational number concepts. Teachers also discussed the use of the MiC ancillary materials *Number Tools* (van Galen, van den Heuvel-Panhuisen, & Pligge, 1998) to support students' thinking in lessons related to rational number. Teachers learned about MiC end-of-unit assessments through scoring and discussing student responses on the assessment for *More or Less* (Keijzer, van den Heuvel-Panhuizeln, Wijers, Shew, Brinker, Pligge, Shafer, & Brendefur, 1998). Sessions were also devoted to the geometry and statistics strands. Throughout the institutes, teachers openly used multiple ways to solve problems and talked about explicit and implicit concepts in the selected lessons. Teachers raised and discussed a variety of issues including the conflict between mastery of concepts over time and grading; representations to support reasoning; prerequisite knowledge for using MiC number units; managing students who work at different paces; and providing meaningful feedback during whole-class discussions.

During the summer institutes, the research team learned about special conditions for teachers in each district such as daily 90-minute class periods for some MiC teachers in District 1 and 120-minute class periods that met five times in a two-week period for some MiC teachers in District 2. Teachers who had some experience teaching MiC prepublication or field-test units readily offered advice to other teachers, and sample lesson arrangements were described for 120-minute class periods. On the final afternoon of the institutes, all teachers met as a group to review study timelines, schedule observations, and discuss teacher compensation.

The research team also supported district efforts to reform mathematics education. For example, in District 1 the district held a press conference with Professor Romberg. Reporters also interviewed a fifth-grade MiC study teacher, who was featured in local newspapers, and video clips of institute sessions were shown during evening newscasts.

In the 1998 summer teacher institutes, new study teachers learned about the study goals and research design, and all teachers heard about preliminary results of student assessments from the previous year. From that point, two concurrent curriculum-specific workshops were held. Teachers who used conventional curricula discussed authentic instruction, tasks, assessments (Newmann, Secada, & Wehlage, 1995) and research on teaching and learning mathematics with understanding (Carpenter & Lehrer, 1999). Teachers read and discussed selected resources and synthesized the ideas into concise statements to be used with their students, which were later enlarged to poster size for displaying in their classrooms.

The institutes for MiC teachers began with a session during which teachers raised and discussed issues related to implementing MiC. Issues mentioned by District 1 teachers were related more to the units themselves such as understanding the mathematics and unit goals. Other items such as effective use of cooperative groups, assessment, and working with parents were discussed, but plans of action were in the beginning stages. The issues raised by District 2 teachers were more concerned with pedagogy relative to working toward the quality of student responses, effective use of cooperative groups, and homework assignments related to particular lessons but from *Number Tools*. Teachers had clear ideas for assessment and work with parents.

The institutes for MiC teachers continued with a demonstration lesson on geometry (in District 1, this lesson was presented by a seventh-grade study teacher). Other sessions included attention to all four content strands. These sessions were different from the 1997 institutes in that teachers at particular grade levels traced development of specific content for each strand, and they presented the findings for their grade level to the larger group. Teachers also discussed possibilities for informal classroom assessment, homework, and the newly developed parent materials. Teachers in feeder-pattern groups worked with consultants provided by the publisher of MiC (Encyclopaedia Britannica) to outline the sequence of MiC units for the current school year. On the final afternoon, all teachers met to review classroom observation protocols and teaching logs.

In 1998–1999, half-day institutes for principals in Districts 1 and 2 were also held. During these institutes, differences in MiC implementation culled from observation reports were described (e.g., teacher preparation, units completed, use of group work, reliance on conventional pedagogy). Student work from study assessments was used to illustrate preliminary differences between MiC students and those who used conventional curricula. Principals discussed organizational support for reform, the use of parent materials, and plans for data collection in the upcoming school year.

In addition to the institutes for principals, the research team supported district efforts to learn about the effect of using reform-based mathematics curricula. For example, in District 1 the research coordinator shared preliminary assessment results during a meeting with the superintendent, the district curriculum supervisor, mathematics specialist, and assessment team. During the meeting, one eighth-grade study teacher talked about the benefits of using MiC and the emphasis on algebra in eighth-grade units.

In preparation for the 1999 summer institutes, study teachers were asked about the content they wanted to pursue. MiC teachers requested information on classroom assessment and time for preparing to teach units that were unfamiliar to them. Teachers who used conventional curricula asked to learn more about informal classroom assessment and creating assessment tasks and scoring rubrics. Two concurrent institutes were planned around those themes. One group of teachers participated in discussions about what to assess and how to assess; grading assessments designed to tap higher order thinking; designing assessment tasks; and developing scoring rubrics for those tasks. The other teachers worked together to solve unit problems, determine multiple strategies for problems, select problems appropriate for classroom assessment and homework, and discuss end-of-unit assessment tasks. Joint sessions on assessment were also held. Teachers worked individually or together to design and refine assessment tasks. For example, teachers in District 1 created tasks using the context of the drought that was occurring in their state. Teachers also brought in three examples of general scoring rubrics to discuss. They scored a set of 20 student assessments from a task on the end-of-unit assessment for *Building Formulas* (Wijers, Roodhardt, van Reeuwijk, Burrill, Cole, & Pligge, 1998) according to their own scoring principles. The results were compared during an intense discussion of the consistency among scorers, the types of items that should receive more score points, attention to what students were trying to convey in their responses, and translating the scores into grades. Teachers recorded their comments about characteristics of good assessment problems and things to remember when scoring assessments. All teachers convened as one group on the final afternoon of the institute. The teaching log was reviewed, and observations and interviews were scheduled by on-site observers.

In addition to the summer institutes, teachers had access to a toll-free telephone number to talk with members of the research team or members of the MiC development team; a service which teachers felt was a beneficial resource. Teachers also contacted the research team about other concerns such as guidelines for selecting computer software and alternate ways to approach teaching integers (teachers using conventional curricula).

In summary, during the summer institutes the research team met and came to know study teachers on a personal level. More importantly, concurrent institutes for MiC and non-MiC teachers provided ways to engage teachers in specific discussions related to the curricula they taught. While MiC teachers had opportunities to develop an in-depth understanding of MiC units and the philosophy of the curriculum, teachers of conventional curricula explored teaching mathematics for understanding and alternate forms of assessment. The professional development opportunities varied each year by the teachers' growing interest in changing their teaching and classroom assessment practices. In the last summer institute, MiC and non-MiC teachers worked together in discussing assessment-related topics. The times spent with teachers and administrators in their own districts proved to be important for the research team in learning about the teachers and the challenges they faced in implementing reform and for the research team to support teachers in efforts to change their practice.

Scoring institutes

Two-day scoring institutes for teachers, on-site coordinators, and on-site observers were held in all districts in May (or June) in 1998 and 1999, and in Districts 1, 2, and 4 in 2000. The purpose of these two-day institutes was for participants to learn about and score portions of the study Problem Solving Assessments.

To ensure anonymity, names were removed from all student assessment booklets, and booklets from the different classes were mixed randomly (Webb, Romberg, Shafer, & Wagner, 2005). Assessment booklets were separated into packets of five to eight booklets. A set of packets was randomly selected from each grade level so that participants (referred to here as raters) had an opportunity to score student responses from multiple assessments. For each cluster of items set in a context (typically two to five items), raters were trained for 0.5 to 1 hour. During this training, raters solved the problems in a particular context, and institute faculty (graduate project assistants) presented and led discussion of the scoring rubric, strategy codes (if any), and student work samples for each item. (An item with its accompanying scoring rubric and strategy codes is shown in Figure 4.1.) After this training, raters scored student responses for that context. When all booklets were scored for that context, raters were trained for scoring the next context.

Each packet was scored by two raters. Any discrepancies in ratings were adjudicated by other raters until agreement in scoring was achieved. Raters recorded their assigned personal codes on lines next to each set of items they scored. This allowed the research team to track interrater reliability, which is the frequency at which two raters who scored a particular student response agreed with one another. At each scoring institute, there

Points	Response
2	Correct conclusion: 2 more cars are needed or 8 cars are needed *with* Correct computation, $4 \times 6 = 24$, $29 - 24 = 5$, *or* correct explanation
1	Correct computation, $4 \times 6 = 24$, $29 \div 4 = 7$ R 1, but wrong, missing, or incomplete conclusion: e.g., 5 students are left or that's not enough *or* Correct conclusion, 8 cars are needed, but unclear, incomplete, or missing explanation
0	Incorrect response (Note: An indication of agreement or disagreement with the teacher is irrelevant in scoring this problem.)
X	Nonscorable or no response

Code	Description
12	Answer only
13	Uses division: $29 \div 4 = 7$ R 1
14	Uses multiplication: $4 \times 6 = 24$ *or* $7 \times 4 = 28$, one more needed or $8 \times 4 = 32$
19B	Descriptive answer based on problem context
21	Uses drawing *or* diagrams to model cars and occupants
19	Other strategy
90	Nonscorable: non-numerical, irrelevant doodles, unclear, illegible
91	Nonscorable: confused (e.g., "I don't understand," "This is confusing")
92	Nonscorable: emotional (e.g., expletive or "This is stupid," "I don't care")
99	No response

Figure 4.1 Item 3 with scoring rubric and strategy coding, Grade 5 Problem Solving Assessment.

was high interrater agreement, indicating a high-quality scoring procedure that reduced the number of items that needed to be adjudicated. For example, in the first scoring institute in 1998, there was 85% interrater agreement, with 13% of the responses adjudicated one time, and 1% adjudicated multiple times.

During the scoring institutes, teachers talked about the ways students expressed their thinking and how they might work with their students to develop more complete responses. Teachers commented on the value of these institutes, stating that they were "an eye opener" and "very beneficial in understanding how students think about solving math problems". Teachers expressed interest in learning about developing scoring rubrics for MiC end-of-unit assessments, and teachers in District 3 requested opportunities for developing assessments (and accompanying scoring rubrics) for classroom use and reviewing test results for the purpose of identifying students' strengths and weaknesses. When we were conducting the scoring institutes, we supported requests from on-site coordinators to talk with parent groups, district administrators, and principals. For example, in District 3 a graduate project assistant answered questions from parents at the local school board meeting, and in Districts 1, 2, and 4 the research coordinator shared preliminary results from the study External Assessment System and the Problem Solving Assessments with administrators. One principal in District 1 requested a special meeting with the research coordinator to discuss findings about the instruction that transpired in study classes and the factors that contributed to the identified differences. Thus, the scoring institutes provided opportunities for teachers to learn about state-of-the-art assessments and ways students responded to selected assessment items, but the on-site visits also became occasions for the research team to support reform at the school and district levels.

District professional development opportunities

Additional professional development opportunities for MiC teachers varied considerably among the districts (Shafer, 2004a). In District 1, the district mathematics specialist arranged monthly focus group meetings for all teachers implementing reform curricula. At these monthly meetings, teachers explored general pedagogical issues including student-centered instruction, assessment, and use of mathematical tools such as the ratio table. Teachers were compensated by the district for their participation in these after-school meetings. During subsequent years, however, the focus group meetings were not held. As a result the three teachers who entered the study in later years had difficulty implementing the MiC curriculum, which they had never taught. Two of these teachers requested support beyond what the study provided in the yearly summer professional development institutes. The sole Grade 6 MiC teacher without MiC grade-level colleagues in her school had difficulty discerning the alignment of lessons with the unit goals, presenting lesson content, and orchestrating classroom discussions. Many of the MiC teachers in District 1 welcomed the visits from on-site observers, and some requested the opportunity to observe experienced teachers of MiC. Although most study teachers participated in the professional development institutes provided by the study, MiC teachers in District 1 clearly wanted and needed ongoing support and sustained professional development opportunities.

In District 2, teachers had numerous opportunities for professional development. Each school was given six early-release days for general professional development, 10 substitute days for professional development in mathematics and science, 12–18 days of mathematics in-service days (provided by USI or Eisenhower government funding and involving two to six teachers at each school), and three to five days of district-wide mathematics in-service. Teachers also had opportunities to participate in five days of paid summer mathematics in-service. During the second and third years of data collection, MiC teachers in District 2 were additionally given one day of release time per month in order to collaborate on instructional planning. Many teachers reported that these collaborative times were very effective in helping them reform their instructional practices.

In District 3 during the summer before the 1997–1998 school year, teachers participated in a district-funded weeklong camp in which they looked at conceptual development across the MiC units at all grade levels, determined the sequence of teaching the units, and discussed instructional approaches for effectively teaching MiC. In addition, 5th-grade teachers met weekly before school without pay to collaborate on teaching MiC. Throughout the school year, school administrators provided paid monthly evening meetings during which teachers discussed implementation issues and continued their in-depth review of specific units in preparation for teaching them. The monthly meetings continued in the second year of data collection. In the third year of data collection, the focus of meetings changed to teachers' understanding of new state requirements for standardized testing. District 3 teachers came to understand that their schools supported mathematics teaching and learning for understanding, and they built on that support to teach a broad range of content, sometimes also using portions of MiC units from prior grade levels to support student learning of grade-level units.

In District 4, professional development opportunities were provided to all mathematics teachers at both district and school levels. The district sponsored monthly one-day workshops for all teachers implementing MiC for the first time. During these sessions, grade-level groups focused on a particular MiC unit, learning about the presentation of the content and discussing instructional approaches and methods of classroom assessment. In the middle school that participated in the study, the assistant principal for mathematics and science held monthly meetings with individual teachers to discuss such topics as reform recommendations in curriculum, instruction, and assessment; research in mathematics education; and applications of research in classroom practice.

As these descriptions illustrate, the support teachers received for implementing MiC varied by district. Teachers in District 1 had access to far fewer professional development opportunities than did teachers in District 2. In Districts 3 and 4, because MiC was the primary curriculum used, teachers were offered much group and individual support. Clearly, these variations in support and collaboration affected reform implementation, and, therefore, student performance (Shafer, Romberg, & Folgert, 2005).

Summary

The professional development institutes provided by the research team supported teachers as they taught mathematics to a diverse group of students. Concurrent summer institutes for MiC and non-MiC teachers respected their use of particular curricular materials, but enabled teachers to discuss issues at the heart of reform—that they themselves were key figures for changing mathematics education in schools and that changes in teaching and assessment practices were needed for teaching mathematics in depth and for understanding. Scoring institutes provided opportunities for teachers to learn about tasks that elicit mathematical reasoning and communication and to use information from student responses in making instructional decisions. During these on-site visits, we also came to know study teachers on a different level and were able to support teachers, principals, and district administrators in their quest for reforming mathematics education.

The types of professional development programs for mathematics teaching, and for teaching MiC in particular, available to teachers varied greatly in their districts, with District 1 teachers having fewer opportunities for in-depth discussions of curriculum, instruction, and assessment than teachers in other districts. These variations in support and collaboration affected the nature of the teaching and classroom assessment practices for study teachers, and identification of influential aspects of these variables in understanding changes in student achievement over time became an important consideration in our research.

Chapter 5

Examining the role of teachers: background, instruction, and treatment fidelity

When we looked at teacher data by district, we noticed that over the three years of the study, District 1 MiC teachers were less likely to teach for understanding than were District 2 MiC teachers (Shafer, 2005a). This consistent difference between teachers in Districts 1 and 2 raised questions about variation in teacher professional background, use of the curriculum, and professional development opportunities.

Background

Over the three years, 90 Grades 5, 6, 7, and 8 teachers from 19 schools in four districts participated in the study. Most teachers taught at one grade level. However, 11 teachers taught at two grade levels in consecutive years (e.g., Grade 7 then Grade 8), and one teacher taught at three grade levels in consecutive years. A total of 37 teachers in District 1, 28 in District 2, 14 in District 3, and 11 in District 4 participated in the study (Romberg, Shafer, Folgert, Balakul, Lee, & Kwako, 2004). Of the 85 teachers who submitted teacher questionnaires, 60 were White teachers, 17 were African–American teachers, 3 were Hispanic teachers, 2 were Multiracial teachers, and 3 were Other teachers;[1] 66 teachers were female. Fifty teachers had taught for more than 10 years. None of the MiC teachers had taught MiC prepublication units for a full year,[2] but most had some familiarity with MiC, and many had taught at least one unit the previous year.

There were no discernable differences in the range of teaching experience between MiC teachers and teachers who used conventional curricula, nor was there any overall pattern of differences in educational background. Most teachers in both groups had relatively few credits in mathematics.

---

1 The category for Other teachers includes Asian teachers, Native American teachers, and other teachers.
2 The commercial version of MiC was first available in the first study year, 1997–1998.

Recent in-service experience varied greatly, but this was not surprising given that most MiC teachers had participated in mathematics education in-service in preparation for teaching the curriculum. We note, however, that many of the conventional teachers, particularly in the first year, had also participated in recent in-service. All study teachers believed that mathematics should be situated in everyday contexts, students had to know basic skills before they could analyze, compare, and generalize, and students wouldn't learn needed skills if they used calculators. None of the teachers believed that students learned best in small groups. Many were ambivalent about requiring written explanations of solution strategies. Such responses reflect the national debates over student learning in mathematics.

Treatment fidelity

Teachers are the key figures in changing how mathematics is taught and learned in schools, and their pedagogical decisions have a direct impact on student learning. Although the research team provided summer institutes for teachers, occasionally acted as teacher resources, and observed classroom interaction, we did not intervene in teachers' instruction or in the ways their curricula were implemented during the study. Rather, for all teachers we collected data on the ways their curriculum was taught, the number and content of units/chapters taught, use of supplemental materials, decisions they made regarding the curriculum, and the factors that influenced those decisions. Specifically, we looked at treatment fidelity as it might occur under "normal" conditions in study schools. We wanted to document the extent to which the use of curricular materials promoted the intended philosophy of the curriculum taught.

We found that many areas of curriculum implementation proved difficult for MiC teachers (Shafer, 2004a). Lesson content in MiC materials is very different from that in conventional textbooks. Content in conventional textbooks tends to be parceled into two-page spreads, requiring minimal lesson planning after the first time it is taught. Instructional emphasis tends to be placed on warm-up activities focused on computation, review of previous material, direct teacher presentation of new content, and quiet independent seatwork. By contrast, in reform instruction, the teacher selects tasks in the instructional unit that might be completed in one day, but also modifies the tasks to fit the needs of her students in engaging the reform content. Instruction allows for student discussion and both independent and collaborative investigation of complex, non-routine problems. The norms of a reform classroom foster sharing of student strategies and consideration of the validity of students' representations, conjectures, and solutions. Teachers listen to students' reasoning, giving feedback that supports reflection on, and engagement in, mathematics. In reform classrooms, teacher decisions vary, not only in instructional planning on a daily basis, but often within a given class period, guided by what individual students actually understand as much as by coverage needs. Teacher preparation time increases, but it does so to the benefit of the students in their care.

The MiC teachers in this study found that they needed to allow more time than they were used to for students to explore the often complex instructional tasks in MiC units, reason out strategies, and determine solutions—in classroom time very different from that required by the skill-drill memorization work with which many had more experience. Students needed an opportunity to explore contexts, make strategic mistakes, and learn to critique and revise strategies. For many teachers, guiding group work was new, and some thought the resulting conversation and student activity appeared out of control.

During instruction, experienced teachers typically draw on their knowledge of difficulties students encounter as they learn given topics, general sequences students go through as they learn particular content, and potential ways of helping students overcome difficulties. Many MiC teachers in the study, however, frequently talked about their "inability to anticipate the students' success or difficulties" and were often surprised, not only by the complexity of problems their students could both understand and solve, but also by the questions that emerged. Few study teachers had experience teaching mathematics that emphasized conceptual understanding and student reasoning rather than algorithms and procedures, and some were surprised at the "difficulty" in teaching interrelated concepts without resorting to the use of algorithms. They also came to understand that group collaboration, although noisier than they might like, was important, and they soon also realized that cooperative work was more effective when they prepared students for the process, made lists of questions that might facilitate discussion, allowed students to first work independently, mixed groups well, and established clear expectations for group work.

MiC study teachers did feel the need to work on "basic skills" when students encountered concepts they had not previously studied or when parents were concerned about the absence of "traditional" work. When this happened, teachers often supplemented MiC units with traditional materials, but also used student MiC notebooks in conferences with parents to discuss student learning. They chose to be proactive with parents through grade-level parent–teacher meetings and open house nights during which parents could examine units or work through sample lessons.

In these districts, we also looked at teachers' classroom (formative) assessment practice—what teachers looked for and the purpose, coherence, and content of their feedback. When teachers gave attention to mathematical procedures without regard to how students made sense of those procedures, opportunities to counteract misconceptions were limited and were sometimes focused on the superficial features of student responses rather than on the mathematics. Although no study teacher planned in advance how to vary problem structure in ways that would encourage thinking at higher levels or emphasize connections between related concepts, several MiC teachers did use the information gathered to plan more in-depth exploration of the mathematical content or introduce another approach to encourage students' understanding. Despite these changes, many teachers still felt the need for formal assessments and wanted scoring guides for them.

In Districts 1 and 2 we were able to document treatment fidelity in considerable detail by focusing on teachers' instructional practices, the content students studied (opportunity to learn), and how the content was presented by teachers. We created indices for scaling the quality of instruction and the opportunity to learn students experienced in order to compare MiC classes with conventional classes.

Composite index for instruction

In Chapter 1 we described the research model that provided the basis for gathering and interpreting information about the impact of mathematics curricula. The next step was to create appropriate indices to scale the variability across classes or schools with respect to each variable in the model and to distill the information from multiple indices into an indicator or composite index for each variable. The indicators (one each for instruction, opportunity to learn with understanding, the capacity of schools to support mathematics teaching and learning, and students' prior achievement) were then used in understanding the relationships between the variables and classroom achievement. In this section, we describe the composite index for instruction and the variation in instruction experienced by study students.

The composite index for instruction emphasized key elements of instruction including lesson planning, mathematical interaction during lessons, classroom assessment practices, and student pursuits (Shafer, 2005a). Through data gathered in interviews with teachers (Shafer, Davis, & Wagner, 1998) and the daily logs they compiled about their teaching (Shafer, Wagner, & Davis, 1997c), we described seven aspects of planning ranging from students' performance in previous lessons to planning lesson activities that promoted discussion, problem solving, and reflection on lesson content. We approached our study of classroom interaction by looking at specific teaching actions as well as lessons as a whole, and we focused on the ways classroom events worked together to shape meaningful learning experiences for students. Using the classroom observation instrument we developed for the study (Shafer, Wagner, & Davis,

1997a), observers recorded information about the ways teachers promoted conceptual understanding, the nature of student conjectures and explanations, whether connections were promoted, and whether multiple strategies for solving problems were elicited. Observers also looked at the nature of the conversation that occurred among students, the nature of their collaboration, and their overall engagement in lesson activities. From observation reports and brief post-observation interviews with teachers, we also identified the on-the-spot decisions teachers made that affected learning of the mathematics, the information teachers sought in assessing students' understanding, and the nature of the feedback they gave to students in response to this information. Teacher journal entries (collected as part of the teaching log) also provided glimpses of classroom interaction from the teachers' perspectives. In all, we gathered and scaled information about 12 aspects of instruction that occurred during classroom activity.

For each of the 19 aspects of instruction (7 on planning, 12 on classroom interaction), an index was developed to look for patterns of variation among teachers. The data from these indices were distilled into a composite index with the single underlying dimension of teaching mathematics for understanding (Shafer, 2005a). Six levels were identified for the composite index. General descriptions of each level are summarized here:

Level 6: Most reflective of teaching for understanding. Teachers emphasized conceptual understanding, and students' solutions, generalizations, and connections were thoroughly discussed. Teachers frequently posed questions focused on articulation of thinking, understanding mathematics, or reasonable solutions. Classroom assessment practice attended to problem solving and reasoning. Feedback that emphasized making sense of mathematics and solution strategies was provided by teachers and students.

Level 5: Reflective of teaching for understanding. Teachers emphasized conceptual understanding, and the mathematical work was shared by students and their teacher. Classroom assessment practices focused on student explanations of reasoning and procedural understanding. Feedback was consistent with Level 6.

Level 4: Attempted to teach mathematics for understanding. Teachers attempted to teach for understanding, but most lessons focused on procedural understanding. Students generally accepted and used procedures presented by their teachers, although they were encouraged to develop their strategies. Teachers supplemented texts with additional exercises, mini-lessons, contexts, or review. Classroom assessment practice focused on student explanations regarding procedural understanding. Teacher feedback was related to concepts and contexts, and student–student feedback consisted of answers and steps in procedures.

Level 3: Limited attention to conceptual understanding. Limited attention was given to teaching for understanding. Students generally used procedures presented by their teachers. Some attention was given to articulation of thinking and reasonable solutions, and teachers occasionally added a different context or review. Evidence from homework, classwork, and at times student explanations was used in classroom assessment practice. Teacher feedback was related to concepts, contexts, and procedures, and student–student feedback consisted of sharing answers.

Level 2: Focus on procedures. Students were expected to accurately use procedures demonstrated by their teachers. Limited changes were made in response to student difficulties or misunderstandings. Evidence from homework and classwork was used in classroom assessment practice. Teacher feedback emphasized procedures, and student–student feedback was minimal.

Level 1: Underdeveloped lessons. No formal lessons were presented. Procedures were demonstrated to individual students, and students depended on their teachers to do the mathematical work. Frequent confusion or misunderstandings were evident, but teacher feedback was inattentive to these, and student–student feedback was nonexistent.

To illustrate the levels of the composite index for instruction, we describe the teaching of MiC teachers Ms LaSalle and Ms Lee, and Conventional teacher Mr Fulton. Ms LaSalle's instruction exemplified teaching at Level 6, which is illustrated in this description of a lesson on May 19, 1998 using the MiC 5th-grade number unit *Measure for Measure* (Gravemeijer, Boswinkel, Meyer, & Shew, 1997). In the lesson, students were asked to determine the amount of castor oil on each of several measuring sticks and to express the amount using both a common fraction and Egyptian symbols. At the beginning of the lesson, Ms LaSalle read a definition of castor oil and discussed its uses. She related oil from castor beans to oil from coffee beans. When she introduced measuring sticks, Ms LaSalle talked about how measuring sticks were used in measuring the oil level in cars. She then used two soda cans to demonstrate the use of measuring sticks. Students were asked to determine the part of each can that was filled with soda. One can was about one-fourth full while the other was about two-thirds full. When the soda was poured into one can, one student estimated that the amount was eleven-twelfths because it was almost full. Ms LaSalle then distributed whiteboards to each group, and students were given five minutes to work on problem 5. Each group wrote their solution on their whiteboard and presented it to the class. Ms LaSalle encouraged students to develop their own strategies to solve problems. For example, the observer noted that one group found common denominators and added the fractions while another group used an area model with rectangles. Similarly, the groups worked on problem 7 and discussed their solutions as a large group. Ms LaSalle worked with students to build discussion, as the observer noted: "[Ms LaSalle] asks meaningful questions to keep the discussion on track". On this occasion, the demonstration Ms LaSalle used promoted understanding of measurement, estimation with fractions, and solving problems with fractions. Ms LaSalle introduced activities but allowed students to solve the problems on their own. She provided visual cues (measuring and combining liquid in soda cans), but she did not interject comments that might reduce students' cognitive activity in subsequent group work. She supported their mathematical reasoning, but students still had the opportunity to develop their own solutions, record them, and present them to the class. Students worked toward sense-making and often provided feedback to each other.

In contrast, instruction presented by MiC teacher Ms Lee illustrates instruction at Level 3, which is described through a lesson on November 12, 1997 using the MiC 6th-grade algebra unit, *Expressions and Formulas* (Gravemeijer, Roodhardt, Wijers, Cole, & Burrill, 1998). In the lesson, students were to investigate ways to give change when purchasing items, to learn about the "small-coins-and-bills-first" method to give change, and to use arrow language in recording their work. Ms Lee began the lesson with a discussion about cashiers in stores giving customers change. She asked whether the students paid attention to ways cashiers counted change for their customers. The first lesson problem asked students to figure the correct change in a given situation without using pencil and paper or a calculator, but Ms Lee proceeded to teach them the standard algorithm of lining up the decimal points when subtracting. She requested that students use arrow language before they had an opportunity to analyze strategies for making change. By directing the way students thought about the problem situation, she focused their attention on procedural understanding rather than linking conceptual and procedural understanding. She presented a procedure, and students were expected to follow it. As evidence of student learning, only answers were sought. When incorrect responses were given, other students were immediately asked to provide correct answers, and incorrect responses were not discussed. Thus, the lesson resembled conventional classroom instruction in mathematics, even when using MiC.

Some teachers who used conventional materials taught in more reform-oriented ways. This is illustrated with instruction by Mr Fulton in a lesson on April 3, 1998 involving operations with decimals. Mr Fulton began the lesson with a discussion of a quiz on decimals. Students gave answers and explanations for the procedures they used, such as "You line up the decimals to add them so you keep the whole numbers and the fractions separate". Mr Fulton continued the lesson by asking students where to put the decimal point in the product when multiplying decimals. One student answered, "Count the places to the right of the decimal in the problem and come in from the right in the answer that many places". Mr Fulton immediately asked why. Another student answered, "When you multiply tenths times tenths you get hundredths", and a discussion followed. Mr Fulton then gave each student a hundreds chart and seven different colored crayons. Students were to use them to color the spaces so that all spaces of one color were connected, list the number of spaces for each color, and make sure that the total number of colored spaces was one hundred. He then instructed students to make a table that included a fraction and a decimal for the number of spaces shaded in each color and total for each column. The class then had a discussion about the equivalence of the fractions and the decimals and their sums. Mr Fulton introduced the word percent and asked if anyone knew what it meant. Responses ranged from "piece" to "average" to "cents" to "piece of a whole" to "part of a hundred" during several minutes of large-group discussion. Mr Fulton also talked about batting averages and how the newspaper misrepresents them as decimals and percents. At the end of the lesson he assigned homework, which was to add another column in the table for the percent of spaces shaded in each color. In this example, Mr Fulton worked toward linking conceptual and procedural understanding of decimal operations and provided situations in which students could use fractions, decimals, and percents to represent quantities in a way that helped them make connections among these representations.

As the descriptions of the instruction in these three teachers' classrooms illustrate, the index for instruction (and opportunity to learn, described in the next chapter) was necessary because we repeatedly found that the use of a particular set of curricular materials does not necessarily mean that teachers' implementation was aligned with the intent of the curriculum developers. In this study, for example, we found that instruction in approximately half of the MiC classrooms in these two districts looked like conventional pedagogy and that in at least three classes using conventional curricula, teachers exhibited reform pedagogy (Shafer, 2005a; Romberg, Shafer, Webb, & Folgert, 2005a).

Some teachers who used conventional curricula were personally invested in the ideas of reform, and some chose to use MiC with non-study classes. Many non-MiC teachers also expressed negative opinions about participating in groups using conventional curricula, as poignantly reflected in comments from one 5th-grade teacher, "We are the lab rats". Ironically, this strong support for reform by a few conventional teachers often resulted in their use of reform instructional practices along with conventional texts, thereby compromising not only treatment fidelity in that classroom, but also the overall findings of the comparative study.

We also found that the elementary school teachers were more likely to support reform instruction, with 8th-grade teachers moving in that direction more than the 6th- or 7th-grade teachers. We also note that the 5th- and 8th-grade teachers were concerned about their students' transition from a familiar environment into a new one (into middle school and high school, respectively). That concern might have been part of their willingness to examine reform materials and practices.

These variations in treatment fidelity underscore the need to go beyond comparison of student achievement scores in studying the impact of a given curriculum. Because variation in the implementation of curricula occurs, descriptions of the alignment of teachers' use of reform and of conventional curricula and respective curricular philosophies are critical in comparative research.

Composite index for school capacity

Another indicator developed to scale the variability across study classes or schools is school capacity, the capacity of the schools to support mathematics teaching and learning. In this section, we describe the composite index for school capacity and the variation found in teachers' perception of school capacity in their schools.

The multiple layers of teaching contexts—students in the classroom, peers in the department and/or school, administrators, local policies, and state standards for education and testing—are also important considerations when examining teaching practices. The likelihood that a teacher will embrace a vision of teaching for understanding, strive to implement the vision, and persist in teaching for understanding is influenced by the work of the school's professional community, a shared vision of student learning, the nature of professional inquiry, and school policy. For example, a strong, supportive, unified schoolwide professional community is more likely to engage teachers and students in pursuing meaningful learning than a community in which no common goals are set for student achievement and no time is provided for teacher collaboration. This collective power of the school staff to improve student achievement is referred to as school capacity (Newmann, King, & Youngs, 2000). Through examining school capacity, we identified and described social and institutional factors that influence student learning.

Despite the professional development opportunities offered in our study, many teachers did not have access to sustained collaboration (Shafer, 2005c). Although they might have regularly discussed curriculum, pedagogy, and formal assessment of student learning, and evaluated new curricula at their faculty meetings, teachers were less likely to have discussed their day-to-day needs: content topics, methods, exercises, and strategies for working with individual students. Teachers were even less likely at meetings to discuss informal assessment and preparation of lessons, projects, tests, or grades. Although teachers regularly talked about parental issues, they less frequently discussed professional literature, their own experiences in teaching mathematics, and mathematical ideas they found interesting. (At least one principal noted, however, that teachers did develop informal ways to collaborate regularly.)

Using data from principal and teacher interviews and questionnaires (Shafer, Davis, & Wagner, 1997a–d), a composite index was developed to scale teachers' perceptions of school capacity. We looked at variables that ranged from the vision for teaching and learning mathematics and administrative support to teacher influence over school policy and collaboration among teachers. Teachers' perceptions of school capacity spanned five levels, three of which are illustrated here with descriptions of teacher perceptions:

Level 5: High level of school capacity. Eighth-grade MiC teacher Ms Keeton felt that principal and teacher visions for mathematics teaching and learning were clearly defined and generally aligned. She felt that she received very strong administrative support in terms of clearly communicated expectations, support for selecting instructional materials, changes in instructional practice, and changes in policy. Ms Keeton felt that she had a high influence in planning and teaching mathematics, an average level of influence over curriculum, and less influence over the content of professional development programs and discipline. She felt that faculty and staff were committed to academic excellence and that teachers supported one another in their efforts to improve instruction. Ms Keeton met regularly with other teachers on her team, and they discussed mathematics content, particular MiC units, instructional and assessment methods, and program evaluation.

Level 3: Average level of school capacity. Seventh-grade MiC teacher Mr Bartlett felt that the principal and teacher visions in the school were aligned on some ideas but were incompatible on others. He felt that he received strong administrative support in terms of clearly communicated expectations, support for selecting instructional materials, and changes in instructional practice, but limited support for implementing changes in policy. Mr Bartlett felt that he had a moderate level of influence over educational decisions regarding curriculum, discipline, the content of professional development programs, and mathematics planning and teaching, but limited influence over textbook selection. Mr Bartlett felt that faculty and staff were committed to academic excellence, although he felt an average level of support from other teachers. Formal meetings with other mathematics teachers in the school were held infrequently, and teachers met informally only a few times to discuss mathematics curriculum, instruction, and assessment.

Level 1: Very low level of school capacity. Eighth-grade MiC teacher Ms Reichers transferred from one middle school to another during the third year of the study. She had looked forward to working with the other 8th-grade MiC teacher at her school, but this collaboration did not take place. Ms Reichers felt that the principal and teacher visions in the school were aligned on some ideas but were incompatible on others. She felt that she received weak administrative support in terms of clearly communicated expectations, support for selecting instructional materials, changes in instructional practice, and changes in policy. Ms Reichers felt that she had an average level of influence in planning and teaching mathematics and limited influence over educational policies related to curriculum, content of professional development programs, and discipline. She felt that faculty and staff were not very committed to academic excellence, and that teachers only somewhat supported one another in their efforts to improve instruction.

As we looked at the perceptions of school capacity for all study teachers, 6th-grade teachers were far less likely to perceive high school capacity than 5th- and 7th-grade teachers in the first year. For example, 6th-grade Conventional teacher Ms Relund perceived low school capacity. She felt that the principal did not have a clear vision of mathematics teaching and learning. However, she felt that she received an average level of administrative support for selecting instructional materials and for changes in instructional practice and school policy. Ms Renlund collaborated with other teachers regularly in informal settings, but no common planning time was provided for them. The teacher leader in her department was a mentor who observed other teachers, provided feedback, modeled instruction, and discussed curriculum and/or instruction with other teachers. No in-service workshops were offered for teachers at the school, but substitute time was allotted for external professional development. District and state standardized tests significantly influenced instruction, as large amounts of time were devoted to test preparation.

In the second year, one-half of the study teachers (all middle school) perceived high school capacity, and in the third year, 8th-grade teachers were more likely than 7th-grade teachers to perceive high school capacity. In Year 2, for instance, 6th-grade MiC teacher Ms Redling perceived high school capacity. She felt that the principal and teachers had visions of teaching and learning mathematics that were aligned on some ideas, but were incompatible on others. She felt that she received very strong administrative support in terms of clearly communicated expectations, and support for selecting instructional materials and changes in instructional practice and policy. Ms Redling felt that she had a high level of influence over educational policies related to curriculum, content of professional development programs, and discipline, and a high level of influence in planning and teaching mathematics. She felt that faculty and staff were committed to academic excellence. Numerous professional development opportunities were available in the school, and the principal also allotted substitute time for external professional development. During formal meetings, mathematics teachers on her teaching team discussed content, instructional and assessment methods, and program evaluation. Teachers also met informally to talk about a variety of topics.

We also found that MiC teachers tended to perceive higher levels of school capacity than conventional teachers, and District 1 teachers were less likely to perceive high levels of school capacity than teachers in Districts 2, 3, and 4. Furthermore, we found that when teachers implemented MiC in isolation in their schools, particularly at Grade 6, student achievement on study assessments remained the same or modestly declined. However, student performance increased when teachers regularly collaborated in meaningful discussions about mathematics curriculum, instruction, and assessment (Shafer et al., 2005). Thus, differences in teachers' perceptions of school capacity helped us to identify other factors that affected student achievement.

Summary

Although there were no discernable differences in teaching experience and educational background among study teachers, it was clear in examination of instruction under "normal" conditions that teachers varied in treatment fidelity—the extent to which their implementation of a curriculum aligns with the intended philosophy of the curriculum. In this study, we found that some MiC teachers used more conventional instructional methods while a few teachers using conventional curricula used reform-oriented methods. We also found that the elementary school teachers were more likely to support reform instruction than middle school teachers, and District 2 MiC teachers were more likely to teach for understanding than were District 1 MiC teachers. However, teachers in District 1 had fewer professional development opportunities than teachers in the other districts, and teachers in District 1 were less likely to feel a high level of support for mathematics teaching and learning.

When a school's staff shares a vision for student learning and develops a clear plan to implement reforms, teachers are able to comfortably work to achieve school or district goals and create classroom cultures that support student learning with understanding. Any unease generated by the implementation of unfamiliar teaching practices is clearly minimized when teachers feel they are working in concert with their principal's vision, and they often more freely dedicate themselves to these changes when they feel the principal's (or the district administrator's) support. Staff (or district) consensus, however, does not necessarily center on teaching mathematics for understanding. When consensus supports status quo, reform efforts can be undermined and traditional teaching practices and goals reinforced. When teachers and administrators share visions of the creation of classroom opportunity to learn that sustains high cognitive demands on students coupled with high expectations of student achievement, high achievement and greater understanding of mathematics by all students is more likely to occur.

Chapter 6

Linking instruction and student opportunity to learn with understanding

In our study, opportunity to learn (OTL) has been interpreted more broadly than its more typical use as a gauge of content coverage. When the aim of the lesson is primarily coverage of content, the emphasis on (usually) unconnected pieces of information reduces the cognitive demand on students. To learn mathematics in ways that enable students to use that knowledge outside familiar problem contexts, students need the time and opportunity to explore relationships among mathematical ideas, to extend and apply these ideas in new situations, to reflect on and articulate their thinking, and to make mathematical knowledge their own (Carpenter & Lehrer, 1999). In other words, they need to understand the algorithms they apply—to understand, for instance, that although comparing shadows of two vertical objects would give a good estimation of height ratio, comparing shadows of the leaning Tower of Pisa and a vertical flag pole next to it would not.

Overall, we found considerable variation in the number (one to nine) and the content of MiC units taught by each teacher during each year of data collection (Shafer, 2004a). Some teachers used units from more than one grade level or chose to emphasize one or two content strands, particularly number and algebra. The amount of time devoted to teaching a particular unit varied from the prescribed 3–4 week period up to 10 weeks per unit. In some cases, units were not taught in the sequence recommended in teacher support materials or were sequenced to correspond to themes common across all subject areas. In fact, teachers found that they couldn't "wing it", but needed to "stick to" the suggested sequence of units and work through units ahead of time to "know where the unit was heading". Yet they came to trust that concepts would be formalized over time, with some concepts initially showing up earlier in MiC than in traditional textbooks.

MiC teachers at various grade levels used instructional materials and methods that were counter to reform practices (Shafer, 2004a; Shafer, 2005b). For example, despite the trend in teaching for understanding among 5th-grade teachers, they often preferred that students learned traditional algorithms for fraction operations before using the MiC fraction units. For instance, in District 1, 5th-grade MiC teacher Ms Mitchell stated that although she was pleased with MiC, in past years she was well known for helping students master operations with fractions by the time they finished 5th grade (Interview, 4/9/98). She expressed concern that there was not enough practice in the 5th-grade number units for students to master these skills. Mastery of fraction operations at this grade level conflicts with the intent of MiC to build on students' intuitive knowledge of fractions, introduce tools such as the fraction bar and ratio table to support their thinking about fraction operations, and revisit and extend these operations to more abstract forms in 6th- and 7th-grade units. Ms Mitchell hoped that students retained the understandings about fractions that they had an opportunity to learn in 5th grade with MiC as they moved into middle school. In District 3, 6th-grade MiC teacher Mr Tierney was not a supporter of a mathematics program that relied solely on MiC. He felt that MiC was only one part of a triad that also included building connections between concepts and procedures and practicing mathematics skills in real life (Interview, 3/20/98).

We also found that two 6th- and 7th-grade teachers in District 1 switched to conventional materials and practices when they thought that students were too hard to control during group activities. Eighth-grade teachers, whether or not it affected their practice, generally felt pressure to use conventional algebra materials to help their students make the transition to traditional high-school mathematics.

Individual teachers can have a very strong effect on the learning and achievement of their students (Shafer et al., 2005). For example, the performance of many MiC students dropped when some MiC teachers devoted little time to MiC instructional units, relying instead on more conventional materials. A detailed listing of the time allotted to instructional activities on September 15, 1999 for 7th-grade MiC teacher Ms Carlson illustrates this tendency to attend to multiple concerns in a single lesson. Students worked in pairs on a review set, for which they were to write everyday items in "simplest form" such as 50 pennies = 50¢ and 24 eggs = 2 dozen (7 minutes). This was followed by a whole-class spin-off discussion of metric prefixes, including a demonstration with a meter stick (9 minutes) and pp. 11–15 in the MiC unit (9 minutes). During the next 80 minutes, students had five assignments to complete: six students at a time on a computer-based skills test until they obtained a predetermined level of proficiency; a traditional worksheet on place value; a worksheet on arrow language from the MiC supplementary resource *Number Tools*; two pages from a resource on solving equations using manipulatives; and pp. 11–15 in the MiC unit. In this lesson, little class time was actually devoted to the MiC lesson assigned for that day, and most of it was completed independently as part of an eclectic assortment of instructional activities with the hope of better preparing students for the state standardized test-ing program and traditional high-school algebra. Furthermore, in the spring of 2000, when it was time for students to complete study assess-ments in Grade 8, Ms Carlson believed that her "at risk" students were not capable of concentrating long enough to take study assessments. Many of her students protested at having to take assessments that were not counted as part of their course grades and often wrote comments such as "I don't know" or "I don't understand" rather than making reasoned attempts at solving assessment items.

In previous studies of OTL, researchers looked at the content of lessons over time, without regard for type or the alignment of curriculum imple-mentation with intended curricular philosophies. In other studies that con-trasted the performance of students who used reform-based curricula with those who used other curricula on state-mandated standardized tests, the ways teachers used curricular materials were not considered. In our study, the in-depth investigation of implementation is one of the ways that differentiates it from other studies of reform-based curricula. We re-described OTL as a student's opportunity to learn mathematics *with understanding* (OTL*u*), and we created an indicator or composite index for this variable (Shafer, 2005b). OTL*u* was characterized through curricular content, the teacher's decisions in defining the actual curriculum, and the development of conceptual understanding through the teacher's active support of classroom interactions that promote students' conjectures and students' exploration of connections within mathematics and between mathematics and their life experiences.

Composite index for opportunity to learn with understanding (OTL*u*)

In Chapter 1 we described the research model that provided the basis for gathering and interpreting information about the impact of mathematics curricula. Along with the model, indices were created for each variable to scale the variability across classes or schools with respect to each variable. Information from these indices was distilled into indicators that were then used in understanding the relationships between the variables and class-room achievement. In this section, we describe the indicator or composite index students' opportunity to learn mathematics with understanding and the variation experienced by study students with respect to this key indicator.

Using data from teacher logs, journal entries, observation reports, inter-views, and questionnaires, an index was developed for each of six aspects of OTL*u* (curricular content, modifications of curricular materials, and four aspects of teaching mathematics for understanding). Data from these indices were distilled into a composite index, and four levels were identified for the composite index. General descriptions of each OTL*u* level are summarized here:

Level 4: High level of OTLu. Attention was given to all content areas, content was taught in depth, and few modifications were made to curricular materials. Portions of lessons focused on conceptual understanding, student conjectures related to validity of particular statements, connections among mathematical ideas were clearly explained by the teacher, and connections between mathematics and students' life experiences were apparent in lesson.

Level 3: Moderate level of OTLu. Although the content was taught in depth, only one or two content areas were taught during the school year. Supplementary activities were occasionally used. However, limited attention was given to conceptual understanding. Student conjectures were related to making connections between a new problem and problems previously seen. Connections among mathematical ideas were briefly mentioned, and connections between mathematics and students' life experiences were reasonably clear when explained by the teacher.

Level 2: Limited level of OTLu. For teachers using MiC, few content areas were taught due to slow pacing, and for some MiC teachers, supplementary materials subsumed the curriculum. Teachers using conventional curricula taught vast content as disparate pieces of knowledge, laden with prescribed algorithms. Few modifications to curricular materials were made, and supplementary activities were occasionally used. All teachers provided limited attention to conceptual understanding, which was consistent with Level 3.

Level 1: Low level of OTLu. Teachers taught vast content as disparate pieces of knowledge, laden with prescribed algorithms. MiC teachers added supplementary materials to the point that these materials subsumed MiC. Teachers using conventional curricula presented content in haphazard ways; no adherence to a textbook guideline was evident. Conceptual understanding was not promoted, and connections were not encouraged.

Overall, we found that elementary school teachers were most likely to promote a high level of OTL*u*, with 8th-grade teachers moving in that direction more than the 6th- or 7th-grade teachers. For example, 5th-grade MiC teacher Ms Piccolo's students experienced high OTL*u* (Level 4). Regarding the content of instruction throughout the school year, Ms Piccolo taught two number, one algebra, two geometry, and one statistics MiC units, and she presented the units with few modifications. The lesson on May 8, 1998 using the MiC fifth-grade geometry unit *Figuring All the Angles* (de Lange, van Reeuwijk, Feijs, Middleton, & Pligge, 1997) illustrates the subcategories in teaching for understanding in OTL*u* experienced by this class. In the lesson (pp. 15–17), students investigated the distortion caused by representing curved surfaces with flat maps. In previous lessons, students used flat maps to locate places using distances and directions. Ms Piccolo began the lesson with informal assessments of students' prior knowledge about the shape of the Earth and history of theories about that shape. Throughout the lesson, Ms Piccolo connected class discussions to the information she learned through this assessment. Using pictures of the Earth in the unit, students described the location of the United States. After this, Ms Piccolo placed large laminated maps of the United States on their desks, and students discussed the location of St. Louis, Missouri as 38°N and 90°W. Students then began work in small groups on questions 2–4, in which they used the map to locate several U.S. cities and investigated whether planes flying in the same direction would ever meet. Ms Piccolo valued students' statements about mathematics and used them to work toward shared understanding for the class. For instance, when students were convinced that airplanes flying north would never meet, she brought out the classroom globe and encouraged students to trace northerly flights with their fingers. This process helped them reconstruct their ideas. The lesson continued with questions 5–7 about the distortion caused by creating flat maps of curved surfaces. Ms Piccolo asked students what would happen to the map if it were pressed onto a large grapefruit that she had brought to class. She cut the peel into sections (along lines of longitude) and flattened the pieces on the overhead projector. In this way, Ms Piccolo provided a visual support for students' thinking, one that students could refer back to when solving problems. Students completed the questions in their groups and shared their answers in subsequent whole-class discussion.

This lesson is reflective of a high level of the teaching for understanding subcategories in OTL*u*. The focus of this lesson was on conceptual understanding. Ms Piccolo introduced lesson activities but allowed students to solve the problems on their own. Feedback was ongoing, addressing student misconceptions through alternative representations. For example, after letting students struggle with the question about whether planes on northerly routes would meet, Ms Piccolo introduced a strategy for students to use that gave them access to the problem and allowed them to pursue a solution. Rather than reducing the mathematical work for them, she opened opportunities for students to think about and explore the mathematical ideas. Throughout the lesson, Ms Piccolo provided the necessary tools (maps, globe) and visual clues (flattened grapefruit peels), but she did not interject comments that might diminish students' cognitive activity. The lesson promoted connections among mathematical ideas (flat vs. spherical maps, number lines, lines of latitude and longitude, geometry, and measurement), and connections between mathematics and students' life experiences (maps, globes, and compass directions).

By contrast, 6th-grade MiC teacher Mr Brown's students experienced a low level of OTLu (Level 1). Mr Brown taught two number, one algebra, and one geometry MiC units, and he supplemented MiC with computer-assisted drill-and-practice programs. This combination resulted in a dual emphasis on basic skills and some conceptual understanding. The lesson on March 16, 1998 using the MiC sixth-grade algebra unit *Expressions and Formulas* (Gravemeijer et al., 1998) illustrates the subcategories in teaching for understanding in OTLu experienced by his classes. In this lesson, students were to use arrow strings to show order of operations. To begin the lesson, Mr Brown asked students to work on pp. 54–58. No expectations were given as to how far they should get by the end of the period, who they should work with, when they could ask a question, and so on. Students were confused because they were not near p. 54 prior to the lesson. Five hands went up immediately, and Mr Brown started moving from student to student. Students waited for Mr Brown to tell them how to do a problem. After that, they asked how to do the next one, and so on. Students depended on Mr Brown to answer all questions and did not move ahead in the lesson until he came to their desks. In some cases, this took a long time. The only strategy they used was the one that Mr Brown explained individually to each student. Students had very little motivation for, or knowledge of, the mathematics they were supposed to be learning. They did not change incorrect answers in their notebooks after talking with Mr Brown, and they just skipped other questions. The focus was on each question in the lesson, rather than on the mathematics students were studying. Each question was treated as a new and isolated topic.

This lesson is reflective of a low level of the teaching for understanding subcategories in OTLu. Mathematics was presented in ways that gave students only a surface treatment of the content. The lesson did not promote conceptual understanding, and inquiry was limited to lower-order thinking. Students began independent work with little direction, and there were no discussions of connections between this lesson and previous ones.

In the first study year, high levels of OTLu were experienced by more classes taught by 5th-grade teachers than students in classes taught by 6th- or 7th-grade teachers, who tended to experience a limited level of OTLu. In the second year, limited and moderate levels of OTLu were predominant for all students, now in Grades 6–8. In the final study year, moderate to high levels of OTLu were experienced by more than half of the 8th-grade groups, in comparison to a limited level of OTLu in classes of more than half of the 7th-grade teachers.

Although the OTLu that study students experienced was inconsistent by grade level, it was moderately consistent by treatment. In the first and second years, nearly three-fourths of the MiC classes (and half of the MiC classes in the third year) created classroom cultures characteristic of OTL*u*, compared with much lower percentages of conventional classrooms. Teachers with greater experience using MiC tended to better provide their students more consistent instruction and OTL*u*, and their students tended to show more achievement gains (Shafer et al., 2005). Our findings suggest that the use of MiC materials enlarged and strengthened students' OTL*u*. We again note, however, that observation data clearly show that many MiC classrooms tended to look like conventional programs of instruction and that a few classrooms using conventional textbooks looked like reform classrooms.

In Districts 1 and 2, the number of teachers who promoted OTL*u* at each grade level was fairly consistent for each study year, with the exception that more classes experienced a limited level OTL*u* in District 1 in the third year. Beyond this we note that district culture and initiatives can also cause variation in the instructional practices of individual teachers. In District 1, with no strong vision of professional development at the district level, some teachers regularly added competitions, puzzles, and games, while others used computer-assisted drill-and-practice programs. In District 2, the mandated school initiatives, such as 30 minutes of class time devoted to silent reading in every class period in all middle schools and mandatory class periods devoted to using mathematics in the workplace, affected the amount of class time devoted to MiC.

Summary

Individual MiC teachers often included non-curriculum-associated supplementary activities or lessons that often compromised the effect of MiC through promotion and valuation of drill-and-practice exercises or lack of belief in student capacity to understand. Interestingly, we also found that some non-MiC teachers supplemented conventional texts with reform materials that promoted conceptual understanding and emphasized mathematical problem solving, reasoning, and communication. In this study, the nature of the modifications made to curricular materials during instruction was considered and instructional emphases were documented on individual teachers.

By linking teachers' decisions in defining the actual curricular content with classroom interactions that promote teaching mathematics for understanding, we were able to differentiate variation in the OTL*u* students experienced. Coupled with descriptions of teachers' perceptions of the capacity of their schools to support mathematics teaching and learning, these variables allowed us to explore factors that influenced changes in student achievement over time. These factors are described in detail in later chapters.

Chapter 7

Looking at assessment instruments

As expressed in Chapter 1, the use of a broad set of instruments is essential for summative evaluations, and the instruments should reflect the curriculum's goals. The goal of instruction using MiC is that students will acquire knowledge of concepts in the four content domains (number, algebra, geometry, and statistics/probability), apply their knowledge in various situations, and develop favorable attitudes. In this chapter, we look at the sets of assessment instruments that were used in this research to empirically document these different aspects of student performance: two assessment systems created to measure mathematical competence, district-administered standardized tests, an instrument to measure student attitudes, and profiles of mathematical reasoning.

Assessment systems

In this study, we created two assessment systems, each with four grade-specific assessments to provide a measure of mathematical competence that could be used as a cross-district standard for assessment: the External Assessment System (EAS) and the Problem Solving Assessments (PSA). The EAS and the PSA instruments were administered to study students in all four research districts in the spring of each study year.

The EAS instruments, one for each grade level, were created to assess different aspects of students' understanding of mathematics. Each of the four instruments was composed of publicly released tasks from the 1992 NAEP, 1996 NAEP, and the TIMSS (Webb et al., 2005), thus, allowing us to relate student performance in this study to representative national and international samples of students. Although student performance on such tests offers limited views of student understanding, this type of test is generally used as evidence of a program's effectiveness. Seventy percent of the items were multiple-choice; the rest were constructed response. Responses on the constructed-response items were scored with the rubrics from the NAEP or TIMSS.

Each EAS contained 28 items evenly divided among four strands:

Table 7.1 Difficulty rating of items by grade level for the External Assessment System

		Number of items			
Rating	Mean p-value	Grade 5	Grade 6	Grade 7	Grade 8
Easy	64	8	6	2	0
Anchor	40	20	20	20	20
Difficult	24	0	2	6	8

number, geometry, algebra, and statistics and probability. Five items in each content strand, referred to as anchor items, were used on each grade level assessment to monitor growth in student achievement over time. Also, two (non-anchor) items in each strand were included in each assessment; these items increased in difficulty from 5th to 8th grade. The p-values for easy, anchor, and difficult items on the assessment were 64.0, 40.0, and 24.2, respectively (see Table 7.1).

The EAS item in Figure 7.1 is a typical anchor item that assessed students' abilities to calculate (multiply and subtract) with whole numbers and fractions, and select the correct answer.

Four PSAs, one for each grade, were constructed for the study by the Freudenthal Institute under a subcontract (Dekker et al., 1997–1998). The format for all items was constructed-response. All answers were scored on the quality of the response (partial credit scoring), and some answers were coded for the strategy used. The PSAs were designed to align with the general reform curricular goals of problem solving, communication, reasoning, and connections (Webb et al, 2005). Sets of items in four strands (number, algebra, geometry, statistics and probability) were non-curriculum-specific, associated with a given problem context, and designed to be accessible on a range of reasoning and strategy levels. Directions explicitly requested that students demonstrate how they arrived at their solutions. Decreasing emphasis was given to number concepts as the grade levels increased.

Strategy codes were assigned when PSA items required that students show and/or explain their work or provide justification for their

Two groups of tourists each have 60 people. If ¾ of the first group and ⅔ of the second group board buses to travel to a museum, how many more people in the first group board buses than in the second group?

A) 2   B) 4   C) 5   D) 40   E) 45

Figure 7.1 Anchor item from the External Assessment System.

conclusions. Codes were created for computational strategies including algorithms, flexible use of numbers, drawings, and tables; explanations and descriptions; use of patterns; algebraic strategies; geometric and measurement strategies; and justifications. Codes were also used to classify incorrect strategies such as arbitrary calculation in which numbers given in the item were used without demonstrating an understanding of the mathematics necessary to successfully complete a solution. Strategy codes captured the variation in student responses, yet at the same time, provided consistency in coding across grade levels. The item in Figure 7.2 from the Grade 6 PSA assesses students' abilities to use a formula; calculate (multiply and subtract) with whole and decimal numbers; use order of operations; provide correct answer; and show appropriate supporting work.

Classroom achievement progress map

We contracted with the Australian Council for Educational Research to develop a single progress map from EAS and PSA student responses as an index of mathematical competence, which we have labeled Classroom Achievement (Turner & O'Connor, 2005). The approach taken to developing this progress map for middle school mathematics follows a well-established methodology, developed and used successfully in a large number of educational research projects. A progress map describes the nature of development (progress or growth) in an area of learning—knowledge, skills and understandings in the sequence in which they typically develop. It provides the framework against which student development is monitored (Masters & Forster, 1996).

Frameworks of this kind usually are developed in one of two ways: "top-down" or "bottom-up". Top-down approaches require specialists to use their professional knowledge to develop a picture of the sequence in which the knowledge, skills and understandings of a learning area typically

---

When you know the weight of a swan at the beginning of a flight—the starting weight in kilograms—you can compute the landing weight with the following formula:

landing weight = starting weight – N × 0.1

In this formula the landing weight is the weight in kilograms after a flight of **N** hours.

11. If a swan has a starting weight of 10.5 kilograms, how much will it weigh after flying 7 hours? Show your work.

Figure 7.2 Assessment item from the Grade 6 Problem Solving Assessment.

develop. For this study we used the mathematics framework developed by the Organisation for Economic Co-Operation and Development (OECD) for the Program for International Student Assessment (PISA; OECD, 1999) and a paper on mathematical literacy by Romberg (2001). Bottom-up approaches use only observations of students' responses to develop a picture of increasing understanding. To create the Classroom Achievement (CA) index, Item Response Theory (IRT) was used to develop objective measures of student progress (Rasch, 1960; Masters, 1982). In IRT, responses to items on a test are accounted for by a single latent trait. Using the IRT mathematical model, tasks and students are placed on the same scale—tasks at their difficulty location and students at their ability location. The progress maps created for the longitudinal study contain six bands. The description for each band includes degree of mathematization, degree of formalization, and the competency class of student work. General descriptions of each band are:

Band 6: Students typically need to identify the key elements of the problem, show an extensive working solution, and provide a summative statement in response to the problem. Students are typically required to identify, compare or combine elements of the problem, draw on assumptions based on real-world knowledge, and provide a fully justified conclusion supported by work, explanation, or reasoning.

Band 5: A high level of mathematization is required in order to respond fully to items in this band, as students are typically required to translate contextualized real-world problems into mathematical terms, and then identify and use an appropriate mathematical strategy and a range of tools to solve the problems. Students typically need to provide a correct answer accompanied by a complete explanation of the work needed to arrive at the solution that takes into account the key points identified in the problem.

Band 4: A moderate level of mathematization is required, as students are typically required to translate either a contextualized or a non-contextualized, generally non-routine problem into mathematical terms. For contextualized problems, the solutions tend to depend on the application of a formula or relationship (e.g., proportionality of corresponding side lengths) with which it is expected that the student is familiar. Non-contextualized items also tend to depend on the application of specific knowledge (e.g., recognize an algebraic expression).

Band 3: Mathematization in this band is limited to the application of mathematical tools in order to solve predominantly routine problems and any contextualized problem-solving tasks that generally require only relatively simple computations for their solution.

Band 2: Mathematization at this level is limited to the application of routine procedures to standard or familiar contextual representations of problems.

Band 1: Partial credit items in this band tend to be of the type in which less credit is given when only some of the required criteria are met or when criteria are met but an explanation is lacking.

This progress map is consistent with both the PISA definition of mathematization and with Romberg's view of mathematical literacy.

For reporting purposes, scores derived from the CA progress map were converted to a CA index by scaling logit values, which ranged from −5 to +5, to scale scores ranging from 70 to 520. Logit scores were rescaled to create positive achievement values that were more intuitively consistent with a classroom achievement measure. The following function was applied to logit values to create CA scale scores: (logit value) × 45 + 295 = CA scale score. The distribution and means of CA scores for teacher–student groups was the primary dependent variable in the analyses that are reported in Chapters 8, 9, and 10. Furthermore, the CA progress maps provided pictorial representations of the variable "mathematical competence". Progress maps were useful in monitoring changes in student achievement over time and in comparison of achievement for various groups such as all students at a particular grade level in a particular year and by district, curriculum taught, and teacher/student group.

District-administered standardized tests

Rather than imposing an additional form of standardized testing explicitly for study purposes, the research team asked districts to provide the standardized test information they administered for use in our study. These data included scores from the year prior to the start of the study and for each study year. The standardized tests varied by district: *TerraNova* (CTB/McGraw-Hill, 1997) in Districts 1 and 3, *Stanford Mathematics Achievement Test* (SAT; Harcourt Brace Educational Measurement, 1997) in District 2, and *California Achievement Test* (CAT; CTB/McGraw-Hill, 1992) in District 4.

The principle reason for collecting and using this information was to match the MiC and conventional students and their classes on percentiles at the start of the study. Because random assignment of students or classes to treatment groups was impractical, we used the standardized test data to look for initial differences among study classes. This is the variable Prior Achievement (PA) used in the analysis reported in Chapters 8, 9, and 10. Percentile scores were used for consistency in examining results across the various tests administered by the districts. The assumption was that study classes were comparable to the groups on which the norm-referenced scoring was formulated. Comparison of percentile scores (themselves derived from comparison to norm-referenced groups) could, we believed, be useful in comparing student groups over the three years of the study and might confirm information derived from CA scores.

Student attitude inventory

Prior research on student attitudes suggests that certain attitudes, in particular those related to confidence, self-efficacy, enjoyment, and usefulness of mathematics, correlate highly with student achievement in mathematics, and that high achievement in mathematics and positive attitudes toward mathematics show bidirectional correlation (Beaton et al., 1996; Dossey, Mullis, Gorman, & Latham, 1994; Ma & Kishor, 1997; McLeod, 1992). To varying degrees, students believe mathematics to be difficult and rule based. They believe mathematics problems should be solved in short periods of time, typically less than five minutes, through application of rules and memorized facts. Overall, students enjoy mathematics, although their enjoyment of mathematics appears to crest in their elementary school years and steadily decline thereafter. In international studies, U.S. students reported that mathematics was enjoyable but boring, but believed that with hard work, they could succeed in mathematics.

We note, however, that much of this research was conducted on students who were studying conventional texts in conventional classrooms. Therefore, we designed the Student Attitude Inventory (Shafer, Wagner, & Davis, 1997b), which included two sections: a set of statements written to reflect important constructs related to students' attitudes and beliefs about mathematics and themselves as learners of mathematics, and a section containing four open-ended items that allowed students to provide more extensive answers on their ideas about mathematics and its uses outside of school. We administered the inventory in the fall of 1997 as a baseline and then again each spring of the study to document any changes in attitude.

Problem-solving profiles

In fall 1997, we administered the *Collis-Romberg Mathematical Problem-Solving Profiles* Form A (Collis & Romberg, 1992) as a diagnostic test. The profiles are designed to yield information about the level of an individual student's reasoning and problem-solving ability with regard to a specific problem situation. Items consist of a problem situation followed by a series of questions arranged such that each succeeding correct response requires more sophisticated reasoning and parallels the increasing complexity of structure (and levels of reasoning) noted in the SOLO (Structure of Observed Learning Outcome) Taxonomy model of cognitive development

(Biggs & Collis, 1982). Similar to our use of the spring 1997 standardized tests, we gathered baseline scores on student reasoning using Form A that we could later use for comparison. Form B of the profiles was administered at the end of each student's participation in the study.

Conditions affecting administration of study assessments

Administration of study assessments proved an area of unlooked-for difficulty. Even with summer institutes, scoring workshops, district coordination, and support by study personnel, many students still had to complete study assessments in less than "normal" conditions: in the aftermath of extensive standardized testing, under unexpected administration procedures, or influenced by teacher reactions to the content of assessments (Shafer, 2004a).

In three districts, study assessments were given to students almost immediately after district tests. A 6th-grade teacher in District 3 reported that students completed study assessments after *three weeks of practice* for and completion of standardized testing, and students "were burned out by the time MiC testing came". Eighth-grade students in District 3 endured *20 days* of standardized tests before taking study assessments. In District 4, study assessments were sandwiched between *two sets* of district standardized testing.

Although most teachers followed the systematic procedures developed for administration of study assessments, assessment results were sometimes compromised by teacher changes to procedures. One District 2 teacher devoted extensive amounts of time to instructions for completing assessments, leaving the affected 5th-grade students too little time to complete the items. In the second year, two MiC teachers (one at Grade 7, one at Grade 8) administered multiple study assessments immediately after each other *on the same day*. One teacher told her class that the assessments had been judged to be excessively complex; many students in this teacher's classes simply left many items blank. Another teacher complained that "at risk" 8th-grade students could not concentrate long enough to take these assessments and that her students protested at having to do work that did not affect their grades. Fully, 80% of this teacher's students made no attempt at reasoned responses, with students completing *at most* 4 of the 21 items. In the second year, in the aftermath of Columbine, many classes were interrupted by multiple bomb scares during assessments, with affected teachers sometimes not allowing students enough additional time afterward to complete the assessments.

Understandably (and appropriately), study assessments did not hold for teachers and students the same high-stakes urgency as district-administered standardized tests. However, the frequent and extensive standardized tests did make any further research assessment difficult. Additionally, teacher reactions to the complexity of concepts taught and assessed and their alterations to procedures do limit the usefulness of any analysis based on study assessment scores and suggest that students' scores are not necessarily reflective of their understanding of and ability to apply mathematics. Nevertheless, we do report findings of note in the chapters that follow.

Summary

The data collected from student responses to the items in these four sets of instruments provided the empirical basis for the findings which follow, with the CA index derived from the eight achievement instruments created for the study being the most important indicator of student competence. The other instruments provided important supplementary data.

Chapter 8

Findings about student achievement, question 1: what is the impact of the MiC instructional approach on student achievement?

The data used to answer this question are based on 17 separate studies: eight grade-level-by-year studies, six cross-sectional studies, and three longitudinal studies (see Figure 2.1 in Chapter 2). In this chapter, the findings are first reported by teacher/student groups in the grade-level-by-year studies. (A teacher/student group consists of students in one or more classes taught by the same teacher.) Second, because the teacher/student groups are nested within districts, the findings for the four districts are used to examine the cross-grade and cross-year studies. Finally, because most students did not stay in the same teacher/student group for more than one year, individual student scores are used in the longitudinal studies (Romberg, Shafer, Webb, & Folgert, 2005b).

Grade-level-by-year studies

Eight grade-level-by-year studies were completed: Grades 5, 6, and 7 in 1997–1998, Grades 6, 7, and 8 in 1998–1999, and Grades 7 and 8 in 1999–2000. Figure 8.1 illustrates the distribution of means for the 92 teacher/student groups on the classroom achievement (CA) index using MiC in the four districts in the eight grade-level-by-year studies. There is considerable variation in the teacher/student group CA means in each of the eight studies. Overall, the teacher/student group means on CA vary from 191 to 316, with 25 of 92 (27%) greater than 275 and only 12 of 92 (13%) less than 225.

To check whether the variation in each study was due to differences between districts or due to differences between teacher/student groups within districts, we reorganized the data in Figure 8.1 for each study. For example, Figure 8.2 illustrates both the variation in CA means across and within the 14 different teacher/student groups in Grade 6 1998–1999. For this study, the bi-modal distribution of CA means shown in Figure 8.2 is due to the differences between districts. All three of the groups in District 3 have means above 275. In fact, eight of the groups across three districts have means above 275. Furthermore, four groups across three districts have means below 210.

CA Index	Grade 5 1997–98	Grade 6 1997–98	Grade 6 1998–99	Grade 7 1997–98	Grade 7 1998–99	Grade 7 1999–00	Grade 8 1998–99	Grade 8 1999–2000
320								
310	6			2				
300		2				6	0	
290	1		2	3		1		
280	1,2	0	1,3,5,6		6	5,7		5,9
270		7,8	9			5	2	
260	3,5	7	6,7			3		8,8
250	2,2,2,9		3	0,0,6	4,7,8,9			7,4
240	1,1,2			4,8,9	4	5	0	5,8
230	1,9	1,2	0	5	7	0,8	4,9	
220	2	8			3,7	6	1	7
210		5		7	5			2
200		5,9	1,3,4,9		9		7	
190				1				

Figure 8.1 Multiple stem-and-leaf illustration of the distribution of MiC teacher/student group means for all eight grade-level-by-year studies.

In general, the other seven grade-level-by-year studies show similar results. The teacher/student groups in District 3 scored higher than those in the other districts, and those in District 4 are often lower. But more striking is the fact that in 14 of the 26 district summaries, there was at least one significant difference in CA scores among the teacher/student groups in the same district with the number of such instances varying by district (two of eight teacher/student groups in District 1, seven of eight in District 2, none in District 3, and five of six in District 4). For example, when

	District 1	District 2	District 3	District 4
320				
310	2			
300				
290	2			
280		1,3	5,6	
270			9	
260	7			
250				3
240				
230				0
220				
210				
200	9	1,4		3

Figure 8.2 Distribution of means for MiC teacher/student groups in Grade 6 in 1998–1999 for all four districts.

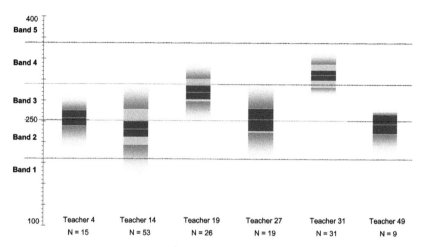

Figure 8.3 Distribution of classroom achievement in MiC classrooms in District 1, Grade 5, in 1997–1998, by teacher.

reviewing the performances of teacher/student groups in District 1 in Grade 5 in 1997–1998, students in Teacher 31's class performed significantly higher than the students of any other teacher, and students in Teacher 19's class performed significantly higher than students of the other four teachers (see Figure 8.3).[1] However, a restricted range of scores was apparent for four teacher/student groups (Teachers 4, 19, 31, and 49). Such restriction suggests homogeneous grouping or tracking of students. This practice was documented in interviews with Teachers 19, 31, 49, and the principal of their school. On the other hand, Teacher 14 taught three study classes, one of which was low in prior achievement. This may have accounted for the greater variation in performance for her students.

Similar constrictions in performances were found in seven other cases. For example, when comparing performances of teacher/student groups in District 2 in Grade 8 in 1999–2000, there was a restricted range of scores for the students in Teacher 45's classes (see Figure 8.4). Teacher 45 was one of the teachers who "looped" with his classes; he moved from grade level to grade level with his students from Grade 6 through Grade 8, and he taught MiC to a core group of the same students all three years.

To explore the connection between variation in CA performance and homogeneous grouping, correlations between prior achievement (PA)

---

1 In each progress map, the mean is indicated by the white line within the 95% confidence interval, which is represented by the black area. The results of 50% of the students are shown in the light gray area, and the results of 90% of the students are shown in each map. When confidence intervals do not align in any way, the means are considered to be statistically different.

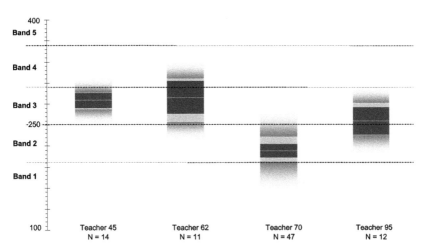

Figure 8.4 Distribution of classroom achievement in MiC classrooms in District 2, Grade 8, in 1999–2000, by teacher.

scores and CA scores were completed. For CA data the first study year, each student's percentile rank from the previous school year was used as the measure of PA, and in the second and third study years, CA scores from the prior year were used as the measure of PA. The analysis suggests a strong correlation between PA and CA performance. For example, in the two cases illustrated above, District 1 Grade 5 in 1997–1998 and District 2 Grade 8 in 1999–2000, homogeneous grouping was confirmed. Thus, despite contractual assurances from the districts that study classes were from average student populations, in some schools students were grouped by ability.

Restriction of variance was not evident in the other six comparisons that showed one or more significant differences among teacher/student groups within a district. For example, in District 2, Grade 6 in 1998–1999, although all classes had similar within-group variations, students taught by Teachers 69 and 85 performed significantly higher than those taught by the other two teachers (see Figure 8.5). The instruction in these classrooms differed. Teacher 69's students experienced instruction that reflected teaching mathematics for understanding. In contrast, Teachers 85 and 52 used non-reform pedagogy, and Teacher 83 emphasized procedures.

In most cases in which there were differences in performance among teacher/student groups, the overall differences were also reflected in performance in each content strand. In a few cases, the differences in performance in one content strand strongly influenced the overall distribution. For example, in District 2 in Grade 7 in 1997–1998, Teacher 20's students performed significantly higher in algebra than other students (see Figure 8.6). Teacher 20 taught one more algebra unit (and more MiC units) throughout the school year than other teachers. Her students' performance in algebra

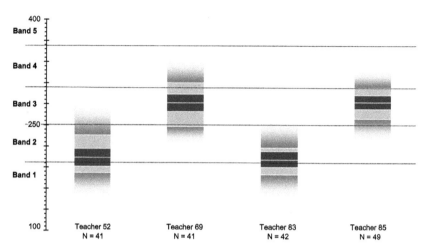

Figure 8.5 Distribution of classroom achievement in MiC classrooms in District 2, Grade 6, in 1998–1999, by teacher.

likely was affected by studying more of the MiC algebra units. These students also experienced a higher quality of instruction than students in the other teachers' classes. (It is also important to note that when Teachers 11 and 35 withdrew from the study early in the spring semester, they used a conventional textbook for the remainder of the year. Given that conventional curricula provide limited attention to algebra, the change from MiC to a conventional curriculum may have had a considerable impact on student performance in algebra.)

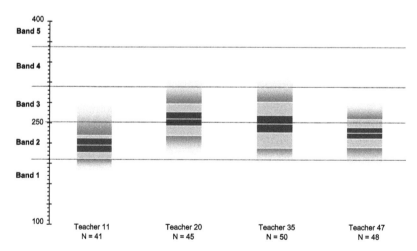

Figure 8.6 Distribution of classroom achievement in algebra in MiC classrooms in District 2, Grade 6, in 1998–1999, by teacher.

In summary, in over half of the comparisons of teacher/student groups in each district in each grade level, important differences in CA performance were found. These differences generally were reflected in the content strands. In some cases, the differences among teacher/student groups showed a constriction of variation due to practices of homogeneous grouping. In other cases, differences in student performance were affected by the quality of instruction and opportunity to learn mathematics with understanding that students experienced.

A second measure of student achievement was used to see if there was consistency with the pattern of student achievement on the CA index. Consistency of performance was deemed important for two reasons. First, since the CA index was created from tests created specifically for this study, the results we found could be idiosyncratic. We used student percentile scores from the standardized tests administered by the districts to contrast with the patterns of CA achievement in all eight grade-level-by-year studies. While the standardized test percentile scores come from different tests and only reflect the students' standing with respect to different, but assumed similar, norm-populations, the pattern of percentile scores for the students in this study in general reflected the variation in CA scores for the eight grade-level-by-year studies, whether one examined the overall variation, variation between districts, or variation between students taught by specific teachers within a district.

Cross-grade comparisons

The CA scores used in the eight grade-level-by-year studies were aggregated to make cross-sectional comparisons of the performance of different groups of students at different grade levels in the same district. The usual underlying assumption of comparability in these studies is twofold: performance will likely increase over the grades and comparison of different groups of students at consecutive grade levels is possible because of the same social culture and schooling practice in a district. In the context of these studies, however, we found both of these notions to be questionable. The issue of homogeneous grouping, the shifting of (usually) students with higher prior achievement to the district Grade 8 algebra initiatives, the high attrition levels of both teachers and students, the clumped distribution of minority students—all undermined the "comparability" of classes within schools as well as schools within the same district.

Cross-grade comparisons in 1997–1998

Cross-grade comparisons in the same year involved different groups of students at different grade levels in the same district. In 1997–1998, data were gathered from students in Grade 5 in Districts 1, 2, and 3, and from students in Grades 6 and 7 in Districts 1, 2, 3, and 4. In the CA scores for the overall population, there was a striking dip in means from Grade 5 to Grade 6, and the scores in Grade 7 were about the same as in Grade 5 (see Figure 8.7). However, these differences in the overall population were attributable to the remarkable differences in means in District 1. In this district, the mean for students in Grade 5 was significantly higher than the mean for the overall population, while the mean for students in Grade 6 was significantly lower than the overall mean. Performance in District 1 contrasted sharply with the performance of students in other districts, who showed improvement over the grade levels. For all districts, performance in the content strands reflected the patterns in the means of the overall population.

The striking differences between the grade levels in District 1 may be attributable to the quality of instruction and opportunity to learn with understanding. Generally, the quality of instruction was higher at Grade 5 than in the other grades. Teachers tended to teach mathematics for understanding, and students participated more fully in lessons. Teachers also taught at least six MiC units, included content in all four strands, and rarely supplemented MiC units with other resources. In contrast, lessons for two of the three teachers in Grade 6 were characterized as underdeveloped or focused on procedures. Some opportunities were provided for discussion during lessons, but student participation in lessons was less than for students in Grade 5. Grade 6 teachers also taught fewer MiC units (one or two units each in number, algebra, and geometry). The performance in Grade 6 rebounded in Grade 7, but not to the level of performance in Grade 5. The quality of instruction and opportunity to learn with understanding varied greatly, with devastating consequences. Because of this, the assumptions for cross-year studies were compromised, and it is unlikely that the changes in performance were good indicators of the impact of MiC over time.

In Districts 2 and 4, increased student performance was evident, particularly from Grade 6 to Grade 7. In District 3, student performance also increased over the grade levels, with a statistically significant increase from Grade 6 to Grade 7. The student population was the most stable in this district compared to other districts. District 3 teachers taught from five to seven MiC units, and 6th- and 7th-grade teachers taught portions of units prior to their grade levels to support learning of grade-specific units. The assumptions for cross-grade studies were likely met in this district. Thus, the results for District 3 students provide some insight into the performance of the same students over time as they study MiC. That is, a positive impact on student performance may occur as students study MiC from Grade 5 through Grade 7.

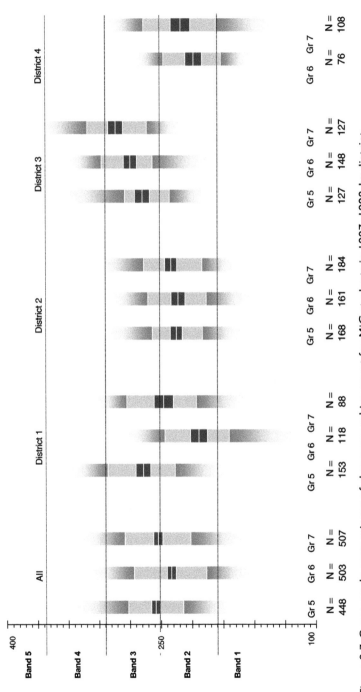

Figure 8.7 Cross-grade comparisons of classroom achievement for MiC students in 1997–1998, by district.

Cross-grade comparisons in 1998–1999

In 1998–1999, data were gathered from students in Districts 1–4 at Grades 6, 7, and 8. In this year, all study students were in middle schools, which eliminated differences in school culture between elementary and middle schools. However, cross-grade analysis for this year was problematic for several reasons. First, the sample of Grade 8 students was smaller in all districts. This situation was largely due to initiatives for 8th-grade students to enroll in algebra classes. This was most pronounced in District 3. Therefore, the sample is likely different from the Grades 6 and 7 samples in prior achievement and other background variables. Second, some students had studied MiC the prior year while other students began participation in the study in 1998–1999. That is, some students studied MiC for two years, whereas others studied MiC for one year. Third, experience teaching MiC also varied among the teachers. For example, half of the MiC teachers taught MiC for the first time, and five teachers taught MiC both years. Fourth, the quality of instruction that students experienced varied greatly, particularly in District 1. Some MiC teachers at each grade level attempted to or taught mathematics for understanding, while others focused lessons on procedures or presented underdeveloped lessons. Teachers who presented higher quality instruction tended to have higher levels of opportunity to learn with understanding. These teachers tended to present content from multiple strands and modified units to a small degree. In contrast, MiC teachers who used conventional pedagogical methods tended to supplement MiC with materials intended to provide practice for procedural understanding. Therefore, the instruction and opportunity to learn with understanding that students experienced varied greatly, particularly in District 1.

There are several interesting findings from analysis of the overall CA scores for 1998–1999. First, the overall CA scores at each grade level were nearly the same (see Figure 8.8). Second, the means in District 1 were significantly lower from one grade level to another. The difference from Grade 6 to Grade 7 reflected the similar pattern from Grade 5 to Grade 6 in the 1997–1998 comparisons. But the performance from Grade 7 to Grade 8 also declined, which was inconsistent with the rebound in the previous year from Grade 6 to Grade 7. Third, in District 2, the means increased significantly over the three grade levels, and in District 3, significant increases were apparent from Grade 7 to Grade 8. Fourth, the performance in District 4 increased significantly from Grade 6 to Grade 7, but significantly declined from Grade 7 to Grade 8. The same pattern of performance was evident in the content strands in each district, with the exception that algebra and geometry scores were lower in District 4 in Grade 8.

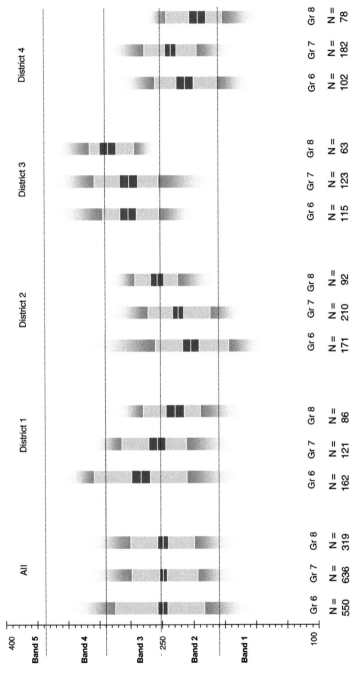

Figure 8.8 Cross-grade comparisons of classroom achievement for MiC students in 1998–1999, by district.

Cross-grade comparisons in 1999–2000

In 1999–2000, data were gathered from students in Districts 1–4 at Grades 7 and 8. Although no new students were added to the study this year, multiple factors compromised the cross-grade comparisons: different student samples (e.g., no students were from District 3 in Grade 8; many students left the study to participate in initiatives to take algebra in Grade 8), the confounding use of traditional algebra texts with MiC by some teachers in District 2, compromises on the completion of study assessments in District 2 in Grade 8, and differences in the quality of instruction and opportunity to learn with understanding in Districts 1 and 2.

The overall achievement scores for students in 1999–2000 across all four districts varied (see Figure 8.9). Given that there were no data for District 3 in Grade 8 and the significantly higher CA scores for the Grade 7 students in District 3 compared to scores in the other districts, it was not surprising that there was an overall significantly lower mean for Grade 8 students when compared with the Grade 7 students. That finding was reinforced by the significant difference noted in District 1, where the scores reflected the differences found in the earlier years. However, in District 2 CA scores were lower for students in Grade 8 than in Grade 7. The overall difference in this case is due to significantly lower scores in the algebra strand. This finding suggests that in Grade 8 in this district, the use of both MiC and a conventional algebra text compromised CA scores in algebra.

As in the grade-level-by-year studies, patterns of performance in the cross-grade studies were checked for consistency by examining standardized test scores from tests administered in the districts. In 1997–1998, the pattern of Grade 5 scores being higher than Grade 6 was also evident in the standardized test data. This reinforces that there were important differences between Grade 5 and middle-school classes.

In summary, the cross-grade/cross-sectional comparisons involved different groups of students at different grade levels in the same districts. The assumption was that the groups of students were comparable because they reflected the same social culture and schooling practices. Given this assumption, increased CA performance was expected over the grades. This was not the finding in these three studies. The comparability of the groups of students was questionable, particularly for Grade 5 students in District 1 when compared with the students in Grades 6, 7, and 8. Furthermore, the existence of algebra classes in Grade 8 coupled with the lack of Grade 8 data in 1999–2000 for District 3 made comparability problematic. However, even when these factors were taken into account, there still was ample evidence of increased performance over time.

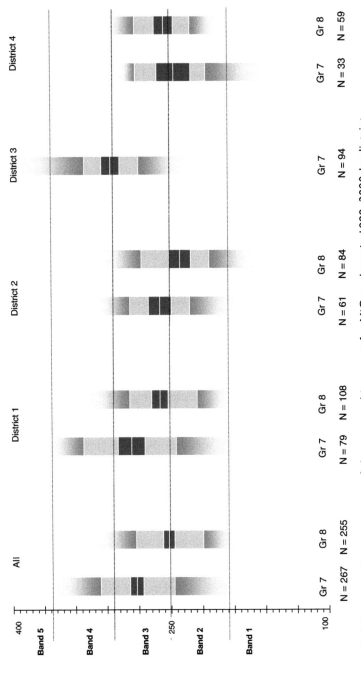

Figure 8.9 Cross-grade comparisons of classroom achievement for MiC students in 1999–2000, by district.

Cross-year comparisons

Cross-year studies compared the results of students at the same grade level in the same district after studying MiC for one year, two years, or three years. The assumption was that students at a given grade level in the same district would be comparable and the results might generate some insights into the performance of the same group of students as they studied MiC over time.

Grade 6 across two years

In both 1997–1998 (Year 1) and 1998–1999 (Year 2), CA data were gathered from students in Districts 1–4 at Grade 6. Overall, the scores for students in Districts 2, 3, and 4 were not significantly different over time (see Figure 8.10). However, the difference was highly significant in District 1, which reflects the findings in the cross-grade studies. It should be noted that students in District 2 were different over time, as students in another middle school were added in Year 2 after teachers in one middle school withdrew from the study in Year 1. By content strand, no significant differences were noted in Districts 2, 3, and 4. However, in District 1 the scores in all four strands were significantly more positive in Year 2.

Grade 7 across three years

In Years 1, 2, and 3 (1999–2000), CA data were gathered from students in Districts 1–4 at Grade 7. The overall scores were not statistically different from Year 1 to Year 2, but were significantly higher from Year 2 to Year 3 (see Figure 8.11). This pattern was also evident for Districts 1, 2, and 3. The means in District 4 increased each year, but not significantly. In District 1, the means reflected the patterns found in the cross-grade studies, and in District 2, results were confounded with the differences in student samples.

Grade 8 across two years

In Years 2 and 3, CA data were gathered from students in Districts 1, 2, and 4 at Grade 8. (No data were available for District 3 in Year 3, and there were different student samples in District 2 in Year 2.) Overall, the scores for students in Districts 1 and 4 were significantly higher, whereas scores for District 2 were not significantly different (see Figure 8.12). The same pattern was reflected in the scores for the four content strands in both Districts 1 and 4. However, in District 2 there was a significantly lower score in algebra in Year 3. This was likely attributed to teachers' use of traditional pre-algebra or high-school algebra texts for part of the second semester.

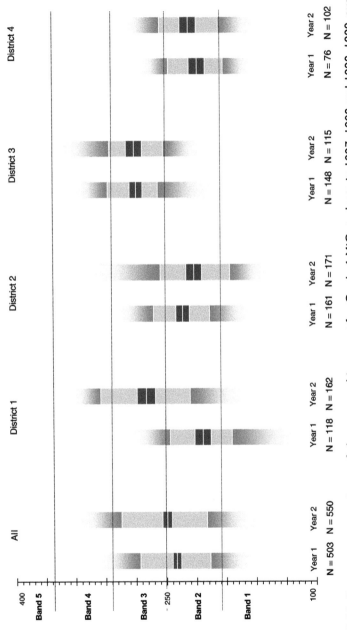

Figure 8.10 Cross-year comparisons of classroom achievement for Grade 6 MiC students in 1997–1998 and 1998–1999, overall and by district.

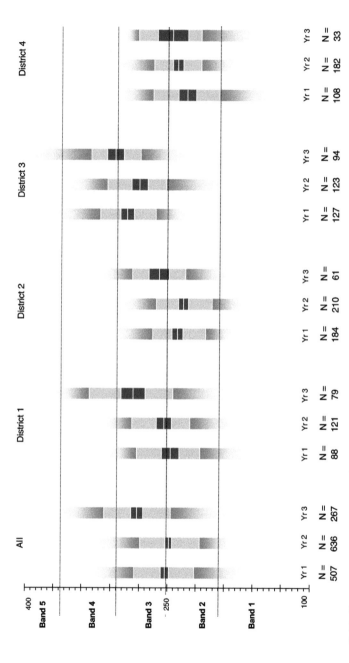

Figure 8.11 Cross-year comparisons of classroom achievement for Grade 7 MiC students in 1997–1998, 1998–1999, and 1999–2000, overall and by district.

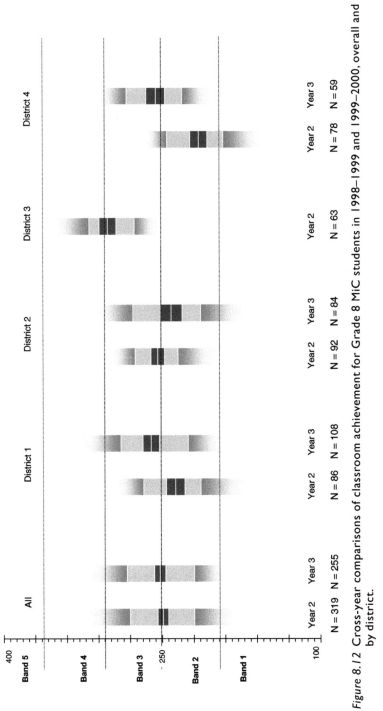

Figure 8.12 Cross-year comparisons of classroom achievement for Grade 8 MiC students in 1998–1999 and 1999–2000, overall and by district.

Patterns of performance in the cross-year studies were checked for consistency by examining standardized test scores from tests administered in the districts. In contrast with CA scores, there was little evidence of improved performance on the standardized test percentile scores. In summary, cross-year contrasts involved examination of the performance of different groups at the same-grade level in the same district across a period of two or three years on the assumption that students at a given grade level in the same district were comparable. We noted that the actual comparability of the groups of students was questionable, given attrition of both teachers and students (in part due to district initiatives), changes in background characteristics of groups studied due to attrition and replacement of study students and teachers, and some striking differences in District 1 that suggested homogenous grouping. In looking at these data, however, we also expected that as teachers became more familiar with MiC materials and reformed their instructional approach over the years of the study, the performance of their students would be enhanced. This expectation was supported in these studies, particularly in the third year at Grade 7. The data also point out the importance of using the MiC materials as intended without supplements from external resources.

Longitudinal comparisons

The longitudinal studies carried out in this study involved examining the CA performance of individual students who studied MiC and participated in the study for two or three years. The assumption underlying this design is that it is possible to track the growth in performance for individual students. Initially, longitudinal comparisons were planned for three cohorts of students, students who began in Grades 5, 6, and 7 in the first study year (Cohorts A, B, and C, respectively). However, the number of students in these cohorts was small, which is attributable to several factors: dispersion of Grade 5 students as they entered middle school; lack of completion of both study assessments each year; withdrawn participation by four District 2 middle school teachers; district mobility rates and parent school choice; and initiatives for students to take algebra in Grade 8. Ten other cohorts were studied as well, which included students who did not participate in the study as planned and students who were added in the second year to increase sample size in each district and to accommodate another school feeder pattern in District 2. (See Figure 8.13 for a summary of the cohorts studied in the longitudinal comparisons.)

Cohorts A, F, and H

Cohorts A, F, and H began participation in the study in Grade 5 in 1997–1998. Because MiC is a curriculum for Grades 5–8, the middle grades

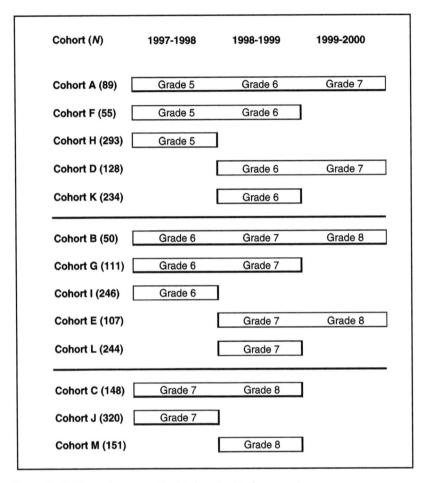

Figure 8.13 The cohorts studied in longitudinal comparisons.

addressed in the NCTM *Curriculum and Evaluation Standards* (1989), the research team attempted to follow students from their initial study of MiC in Grade 5 through Grades 6 and 7. In calculating CA scores, only those students who completed both assessments designed for the study, the Problem Solving Assessment (PSA) and the External Assessment System (EAS), were included in this analysis. Because student responses on assessment items were integral to the design of the proficiency scale for CA, missing scores were not statistically imputed. Cohort F completed study assessments in Grade 5 and Grade 6. In the third study year, however, several factors influenced their lack of participation: both study assessments were not completed in the third year, change in parental consent, and movement to non-study classes. Cohort H completed study assessments only in Grade 5.

The growth in CA performance for Cohort A was statistically significant with means increasing from 271.6 to 282.5 to 304.1 over the three years (see Figure 8.14). In Year 3, half the students were in Band 4, indicating that students solved problems that involved a moderate level of mathematization, translation of a contextualized problem into mathematical terms, and application of specific mathematical knowledge or formulas. Nearly half were in Band 3, indicating that students were able to solve contextualized problem-solving tasks that generally required relatively simple computations for their solution. In contrast, performance of Cohort F, in the study for two years, was much lower in Grades 5 and 6 than Cohort A. The means (265.7 and 268.1, respectively) were in Band 3. Few students were in Band 4, and more students were in Band 2, indicating that students applied routine procedures to standard or familiar computations for solutions, than Cohort A. The performance of Cohort H, in the study only in Grade 5, was much lower (mean 247.4) than the other cohorts, and the differences were statistically significant. It is clear that students who did not continue in the study at the end of Grade 5 (Cohort H) scored significantly lower than those who continued a second year (Cohort F) or those who participated all three years (Cohort A).

Cohorts B, G, and I

Cohorts B, G, and I began participation in the study in Grade 6 in 1997–1998. Recognizing that MiC might only be implemented in Grades 6–8, a cohort of students who began the study in Grade 6 in Year 1 was followed for three years. In calculating CA scores, only those students who completed both study assessments were included in this analysis. Missing scores on either assessment were not statistically imputed. The small number of students in Cohort B is attributable to several factors: loss of students when two Grade 7 teachers in District 2 withdrew from the study in Year 1, initiatives for Grade 8 students to enroll in algebra classes, and lack of completion of both study assessments in Grade 8 in District 3 due to a misunderstanding between teachers at the school. Cohort G completed study assessments in Grades 6 and 7, and Cohort I completed study assessments only in Grade 6.

Growth in CA performance for Cohort B students was evident with means increasing from 215.1 to 247.8 to 252.4 over the three years (see Figure 8.15). From Year 1 to Year 2, the increase in CA performance was statistically significant, and from Year 2 to Year 3 performance only slightly increased. In Year 3, half the students were in Band 3, and the mean performance (252.4) was nearly in Band 3, indicating that students were able to solve contextualized problem-solving tasks that generally

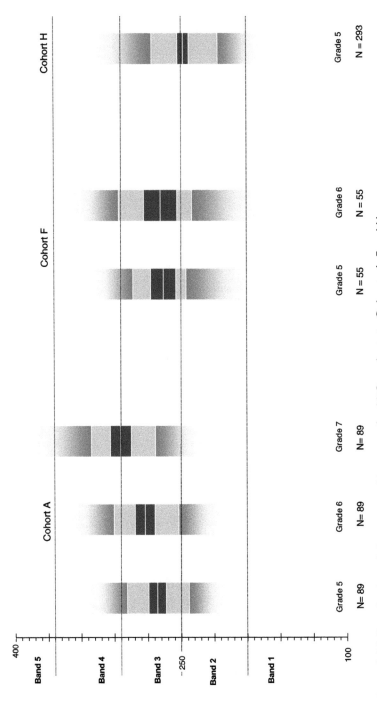

Figure 8.14 Distribution of classroom achievement for MiC students in Cohorts A, F, and H.

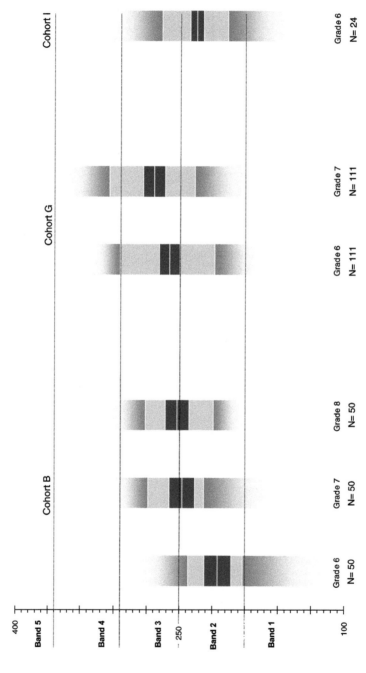

Figure 8.15 Distribution of classroom achievement for MiC students in Cohorts B, G, and I.

required relatively simple computations for their solution. Other students were in Band 2, indicating that students applied routine procedures to standard or familiar word problems. Cohort G scored significantly higher both years than Cohort B and showed substantial growth with means increasing from 259.5 to 273.4. It is also clear that those Grade 6 students who were in the study for only one year (Cohort I) scored significantly lower than those that continued a second year (Cohort G) and those who continued for all three years (Cohort B).

Cohorts C and J

Cohorts C and J began their participation in the study in Grade 7 during the 1997–1998 school year, and Cohort M started their participation in 1998–1999. Recognizing that MiC might be used in Grades 7 and 8 without implementation in Grade 6, a cohort of students who began the study in Grade 7 in Year 1 was followed for two years. Only those students who completed both assessments designed for the study were included in this analysis. Missing scores on either assessment were not statistically imputed. Some of the same factors that affected other cohorts also affected the size of Cohort C: loss of students when two Grade 7 teachers in District 2 withdrew from the study in Year 1, initiatives for Grade 8 students to enroll in algebra classes, change in parental consent, movement of students to non-study schools, or assignment of students to non-study classes.

Growth in CA performance for Cohort C students was nearly statistically significant with means increasing from 251.3 to 263.8 over the two years (see Figure 8.16). At the end of the second year, more students were in Band 3, indicating that they were able to solve contextualized problem-solving tasks that generally required relatively simple computations for their solution. Cohort J completed study assessments only in Grade 7. CA performance of Cohort J was comparable to Cohort C with mean performance at 255.0 after studying MiC for one year.

In the longitudinal studies, we examined the CA performance of individual students for two or three years. We looked at three situations in which schools might plan to use MiC: from Grade 5 through Grade 7, with a transition from elementary to middle schools; from Grade 6 through Grade 8 in middle schools; and from Grade 7 through Grade 8 in middle schools. Although the number of students in the cohorts was small, there were multiple examples of gains in achievement for students who studied MiC.

Students who began their study of MiC in Grade 5 and studied MiC for three years experienced significant gains in achievement, and by the end of Grade 7 half of the students were able to solve problems that involved a moderate level of mathematization. The performance of students who studied MiC from Grade 5 through Grade 6 increased slightly, with most

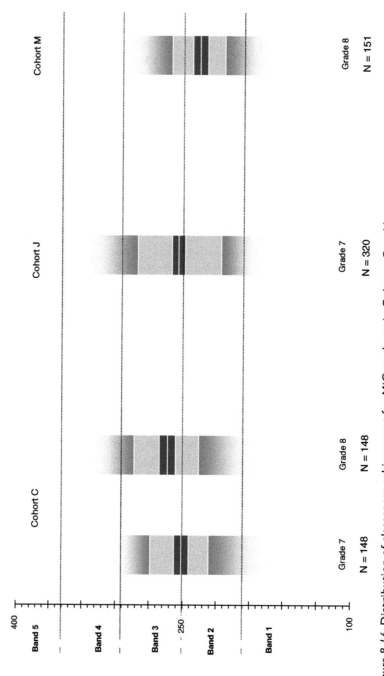

Figure 8.16 Distribution of classroom achievement for MiC students in Cohorts C and J.

students able to solve problems that required simple calculations or routine procedures. Confounding issues for this group included differences in instruction and opportunity to learn that were apparent in the grade-level-by-year studies. For students who began their study of MiC in Grade 6 and studied MiC for three years, significant gains in achievement from Grade 6 through Grade 7 and modest gains from Grade 7 through Grade 8 were evident. The students we followed from Grade 6 through Grade 7 showed substantial growth over time. Also, students who studied MiC for two years from Grade 7 through Grade 8 experienced substantial gains in achievement.

In summary, the number of students we were able to follow longitudinally was small due to students not completing both study assessments each year, placement of students in non-study classes, mobility, teacher commitment, and matriculation into 8th-grade algebra classes. Nevertheless, across the longitudinal cohorts, there was ample evidence that MiC had an important impact on the mathematical performance of students who studied the curriculum for two or three years.

Answer to Question I

The grade-level-by-year studies, cross-sectional comparisons, and longitudinal studies suggest that the MiC instructional approach, as practiced in four school districts in four grades, yielded considerable variation in CA scores when implemented in classrooms. However, there were ample examples of student gains in CA scores in various classrooms. The impact of MiC varied due to several factors depending in large part on the student's prior mathematical knowledge and each teacher's level of implementation judged by the quality of instruction and opportunity to learn with understanding that occurred. For example, MiC teacher Ms Keeton "looped" with her classes and taught a group of the same students in Grades 7 and 8. She taught MiC in an in-depth way with methods reflective of teaching mathematics for understanding, and she taught MiC units throughout the school year in multiple content strands with limited class time devoted to practicing basic skills. This combination of teaching for understanding and OTLu contributed to the performance of Ms Keeton's students in important ways. The gains in students' performance in her classes from Grade 7 to Grade 8 were statistically significant, with CA means increasing from 255.02 to 272.15 (see Figure 8.17). In Grade 8, most students were in Band 3, and over one-fourth of the students were in Band 4 in the statistics strand. Significant differences were also apparent with respect to the number and statistics strands. The performance in the number strand suggests that students' abilities to work with numbers grew dramatically, despite only one 8th-grade unit in the number strand. The performance in the statistics strand reflects the

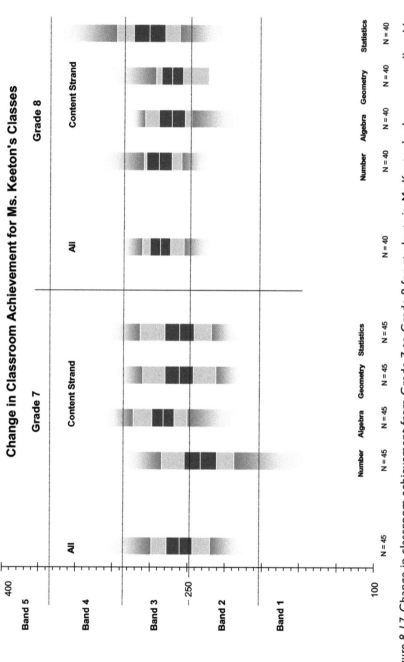

Figure 8.17 Change in classroom achievement from Grade 7 to Grade 8 for students in Ms Keeton's classes, overall and by content strand.

important impact of students' opportunity to learn one of the 8th-grade MiC statistics units.

In summary, the results of the grade-level-by-year studies, cross-sectional comparisons, and longitudinal studies suggest that the MiC instructional approach had a positive impact on student performance. Students' prior achievement and the ways teachers implemented MiC were found to influence differences in the performances among teacher/student groups, and within most teacher/student groups, considerable variance in performance was found. In longitudinal comparisons, students were the unit of analysis. Although small in sample size, the findings from multiple cohorts of students suggest that MiC had a substantial impact on student achievement over two or three years.

Chapter 9

Findings about student achievement, question 2: how is the impact of instruction using MiC different from that of conventional instruction on student performance?

To answer Question 2, a quasi-experimental non-equivalent alternate treatment study was carried out (Romberg et al., 2005a). Data were collected for two treatment groups: students using MiC and students using conventional curricula in the two districts that allowed us to conduct a comparative study, Districts 1 and 2.

Quasi-experimental studies are similar to true-experiments, but they often involve biases that cannot be controlled because of the social difficulties in randomly assigning experimental units to treatments. Consequently, the experimental units are not equivalent. Therefore, differences in treatments and in experimental units must both be accounted for in determining the total quantitative effect after treatment, rather than only the differences in treatments in true-experiments.

In our study, social difficulties existed in randomly assigning experimental units to treatments (Shafer, 2004a). Many districts expressed concern that they might be seen as withholding opportunities for learning mathematics in more powerful ways from students who continued to study conventional curricula. Also, principals and teachers in schools using conventional curricula did not want to be perceived as disregarding district efforts to use reform pedagogy and reform curricula. We found two districts that were willing to participate in a comparative experiment, but the selection of study schools by district administrators depended on finding principals in elementary-middle school feeder patterns who were willing to participate in the research, finding teachers willing to be involved in the data collection process, and finding an adequate number of students with parental consent for each treatment.

The experimental units in our study were groups of students in one or more classes being taught by a teacher during an academic year. We refer to these units as teacher/student groups. Because random assignment of either students or teachers to treatment groups (MiC or Conventional curricula) was not possible, it was imperative for us to examine the actual differences in the two treatments in study classrooms. In the next sections, we describe the differences in both the treatments and the experimental units.

Differences in treatments

Differences in treatments (MiC or Conventional curricula) were explored through studying variation in two indicators or composite variables: instruction (I) and opportunity to learn with understanding (OTLu). In Districts 1 and 2, we scaled this variation using the indices we created and data gathered from classroom observations, teaching logs, and teacher journal entries, interviews, and questionnaires.

Instruction (I)

As described in Chapter 5, the composite index for instruction included multidimensional aspects of instruction in four categories: lesson planning, mathematical interaction during instruction, classroom assessment practice, and student pursuits during instruction. The composite index classified the quality of instruction into six levels with the underlying single dimension being teaching mathematics for understanding: Level 6—Most reflective of teaching mathematics for understanding; Level 5—Reflective of teaching for understanding; Level 4—Attempt to teach for understanding; Level 3—Limited attention to conceptual understanding; Level 2—Focus on procedures; and Level 1—Underdeveloped lessons. We found that instruction for half of the MiC teacher/student groups looked like conventional pedagogy (Levels 1, 2, and 3) and that three teacher/student groups using conventional curricula experienced teaching for understanding (Levels 4, 5, and 6; see Table 9.1).

To illustrate the differences among the MiC and Conventional treatment groups, we contrast the instruction experienced in two 5th-grade

Table 9.1 Level of instruction for teacher/student groups, by treatment

Level of instruction	Teacher/student groups	
	MiC (N)	Conventional (N)
6	3	0
5	14	1
4	11	2
3	14	2
2	9	12
1	5	9

teacher/student groups, Ms Kipling's MiC group and Mr Fulton's Conventional group (Romberg & Shafer, 2005). Ms Kipling presented lessons that were more reflective of good conventional pedagogy (Level 3). She generally presented problem-solving strategies or procedures to her students, and she asked students to use precise mathematical terminology. At times, she expected meaningful explanations and asked students to think about alternate solution strategies. In contrast, Mr Fulton presented lessons that emphasized conceptual understanding (Level 5). Although students tended to give steps in a procedure as evidence of their thinking, he pressed students to talk about why procedures worked and to consider the reasonableness of answers. He modified lessons based on student statements or inquiries and promoted connections among mathematical ideas or between mathematics and students' lives. In other words, the instruction Mr Fulton's students experienced was more reflective of teaching mathematics for understanding than good conventional pedagogy.

Our findings about the variation in instruction in each treatment group indicate one important way in which the experimental units differed.

Opportunity to learn with understanding (OTLu)

As described in Chapter 6, the composite index for OTL*u* included attention to the curricular content taught, modifications to curricular materials, and teaching mathematics for understanding, which included the development of conceptual understanding, the nature of students' conjectures, and students' exploration of connections within mathematics and between mathematics and their life experiences. The composite index classified the OTL*u* students experienced into four levels: Level 4—High level of OTL*u*; Level 3—Moderate Level of OTL*u*; Level 2—Limited OTL*u*; and Level 1—Low level of OTL*u*. Two-thirds of the MiC teacher/student groups experienced classroom cultures characteristic of OTL*u* (Levels 3 and 4), compared with the conventional teacher/student groups, which tended to experience limited OTL*u* (Level 2; see Table 9.2).

To illustrate the variation we found among MiC teacher/student groups, we describe the OTL*u* experienced by students in two 7th-grade MiC groups, Ms Keeton's group and Mr Donnely's group. Ms Keeton's students experienced a high level of opportunity to learn with understanding (Level 4). She presented a comprehensive curriculum, teaching six MiC units in three content strands. Mathematics was explored in enough detail for students to think about relationships among mathematical ideas or to link procedural and conceptual knowledge. Occasionally, Ms Keeton supplemented MiC with activities disconnected from the curriculum, such as practice for district standardized tests. In contrast, students in Mr Donnely's classes experienced limited opportunity to learn with understanding (Level 2). He presented three MiC units in different content

Table 9.2 Level of opportunity to learn with understanding for teacher/student groups, by treatment

Level of OTLu	Teacher/student groups	
	MiC (N)	Conventional (N)
4	20	0
3	19	6
2	16	18
1	1	2

strands and supplemented heavily with drill-and-practice materials. Lessons provided little attention to conceptual understanding, and connections were not discussed.

Although both teachers taught MiC at Grade 7, these teacher/student groups experienced different levels of opportunity to learn with understanding. Ms Keeton's students studied a variety of content in depth with attention to conceptual and procedural understanding. In contrast, Mr Donnely supplemented MiC with extensive amounts of skill practice and devoted little attention to understanding mathematics or to linking procedural and conceptual knowledge. The differences between these two teacher/student groups illustrate another important way in which the experimental units in our study differed.

Distinctions among treatment groups

Taken together, measures of the quality of instruction and OTLu provided insight into teachers' implementation of their curricula. It is clear that the instruction and OTLu experienced by many MiC teacher/student groups tended to look like that experienced in many conventional groups. To further examine this, we constructed a cross-tab of all teacher/student groups with respect to these two variables (see Figure 9.1).

We noticed three distinct treatment groups. The first treatment group, referred to as MiC, includes the MiC teacher/student groups in the top right and left quadrants (Levels 4, 5, and 6 for instruction; Levels 2, 3, and 4 for OTLu). This treatment, which was composed of 28 (of 79) teacher/student groups, reflected the intended pedagogy and content of MiC. The two other treatment groups were rated Levels 1, 2, or 3 for instruction and Levels 1, 2, 3, or 4 for OTLu. In one of these treatment groups, referred to as MiC (Conventional), MiC was taught nominally because a combination of MiC and supplementary materials were used or MiC was taught with

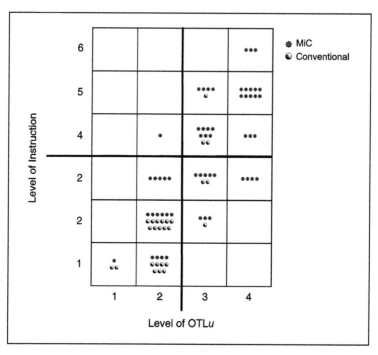

Figure 9.1 Cross-tab of levels of instruction and OTL*u* for MiC and Conventional teacher/student groups.

conventional pedagogy (28 teacher/student groups). The other treatment group, referred to as Conventional, used conventional materials with conventional pedagogy (23 teacher/student groups). In addition, there were three outlier teacher/student groups in the upper right quadrant that did not use MiC but exhibited reform ideas in curriculum and instruction. Because the sample size in each of these groups was small, we did not include them in further analysis.

Thus, based on the ways teachers implemented their curricula (judged by the quality of instruction and OTL*u* experienced in each teacher/student group), we identified three distinct treatment groups: MiC, MiC (Conventional), and Conventional. The data from these treatments are compared in answering Question 2.

Differences in experimental units

The experimental units in our study were teacher/student groups. Each group included students in one or more mathematics classes taught by a particular teacher. Differences in experimental units stemmed from both student and teacher characteristics.

Students

In the eight grade-level-by-year studies (Grades 5, 6, and 7 in 1997–1998; Grades 6, 7, and 8 in 1998–1999; and Grades 7 and 8 in 1999–2000), the number of girls and boys varied, but only one large difference was noted in Grade 6 in 1997–1999 when girls in MiC teacher/student groups greatly outnumbered boys (78 to 59, respectively), and boys in Conventional groups greatly outnumbered girls (73 to 51, respectively). In five of the eight studies, the treatment groups varied greatly in ethnic composition. For example, in Grade 7 in 1998–1999, the MiC treatment group included a large proportion of African–American students and Hispanic students, in contrast to the large proportion of White students and African–American students in the other treatment groups (see Table 9.3).

The number of students in all three treatment groups sharply declined over the three years of the study. For example, in 1997–1998, 403 Grade 6 students participated in the study (137 MiC, 142 MiC (Conventional), and 124 Conventional), but two years later, only 220 of these students remained (76 MiC, 116 MiC (Conventional), and 28 Conventional). This attrition made comparative inferences in the later years of the study problematic.

Prior achievement also varied among treatment groups. For example, in Grade 5 in 1997–1998, the prior achievement of Conventional students (mean percentile 75.6 on district-administered standardized tests) was significantly higher than the prior achievement of MiC students (mean percentile 59.3) and MiC (Conventional) students (mean percentile 60.4). By teacher/student group, the mean percentile scores in Grade 5 varied from 24.13 in MiC (Conventional) Ms Linne's group to 92.37 in MiC Ms LaSalle's group, and both Conventional groups had means over 70. Furthermore, the standard deviations for most teacher/student groups in District 1 were low, which implies that some homogeneous grouping or tracking of students took place in this district, a practice that was documented in principal and teacher interviews for one school.

Table 9.3 Ethnicity of Grade 7 students in 1998–1999, by treatment

Treatment/ethnicity	MiC		MiC (Conventional)		Conventional	
	N	%	N	%	N	%
White	34	18%	60	42%	54	54%
African–American	73	39%	52	36%	24	24%
Hispanic	46	25%	11	7%	7	7%
Other*	34	18%	21	15%	15	15%

* Other students include Asian students, Native American students, Multiracial students, and other students.

These examples make it clear that the students in the experimental units in our study differed by gender, ethnicity, sample size, prior achievement, and the ways they were grouped for instruction.

Teachers

Most teachers in the three treatment groups were female, and most were White teachers. A pattern of differences in the number of years of teaching prior to the study was not discernable. However, teachers varied in their perceptions of the capacity of their schools to support mathematics teaching and learning. As described in Chapter 5, the composite index for school capacity included multidimensional aspects that ranged from the vision for teaching and learning mathematics and administrative support to teacher influence over school policy and collaboration among teachers. Teachers' perceptions of school capacity (SC) spanned five levels: Level 5—High level of SC; Level 4—Moderately high level of SC; Level 3—Average level of SC; Level 2—Low level of SC; and Level 1—Very low level of SC. We found that half of the teachers in the MiC treatment group perceived higher levels of SC (Levels 4 and 5) than teachers in the other treatment groups (see Table 9.4). However, the SC perceived by teachers in each treatment also varied among the levels, which illustrates another aspect of the differences in the experimental units.

In summary, the experimental units in our study varied in several ways: curricular implementation (with identification of three treatment groups); student background characteristics of gender, ethnicity, and prior achievement; ways students were grouped for instruction; and teachers' perceptions of the capacity of their schools to support mathematics teaching and learning.

Table 9.4 Level of school capacity for teacher/student groups, by treatment

	Teacher/student groups		
Level of school capacity	*MiC (N)**	*MiC (Conventional) (N)*	*Conventional (N)*
5	8	3	1
4	6	3	3
3	8	11	7
2	4	9	10
1	1	1	1

* Data were not available for one teacher/student group in each treatment group.

Differences in performance among treatment groups

To answer Question 2, we compared results of the grade-level-by-year, cross-sectional, and longitudinal studies to describe differences in class-room achievement (CA) performance among the treatment groups (Romberg et al., 2005a). We also considered the influence of students' prior achievement and its effect on CA performance. As a result, we were able to formulate a broader set of conclusions about student performance. These findings are discussed in this section.

Grade-level-by-year studies

The overall differences in CA scores for the MiC, MiC (Conventional), and Conventional treatment groups in the eight grade-level-by-year stud-ies are shown in Figure 9.2. In the eight studies, there were ten instances in which differences in the overall mean scores between the three groups were significant: the performance of the MiC treatment group was higher than the MiC (Conventional) group in four studies and higher than the Conventional group in three studies; the performance of the MiC (Conventional) group was higher than the MiC group in two studies; and the performance of the Conventional group was higher than the MiC group in one study and higher than the MiC (Conventional) group in another study. However, the differences among treatment groups were attributed to differences in district performances. For example, in Grade 6 in 1997–1998, the mean scores for the MiC and Conventional treatment groups were similar and were significantly higher than the MiC (Conventional) treatment. A closer review revealed that in District 1 the mean CA score for Conventional treatment group was significantly higher than the MiC and MiC (Conventional) groups, in comparison to the significantly higher performance of the MiC group over other groups in District 2.

The differences in CA scores were also found to be attributable to the performances of teacher/student groups. For example, in Grade 6 in 1998–1999, eight teacher/student groups with CA means above 265 (four MiC groups, two MiC (Conventional) groups, and two Conventional groups) had significantly higher means than the other four teacher/student groups (three MiC (Conventional) and one Conventional). Most teacher/student groups with significantly higher mean scores experienced instruction that attended to conceptual understanding (Levels 4, 5, or 6) or that was more reflective of good conventional pedagogy (Level 3). Teacher/student groups with lower mean scores tended to experience underdeveloped lessons or lessons focused on procedural understanding (Levels 1 or 2). Furthermore, some differences in school capacity, such as time for teacher collaboration, were also found to be influential factors. Therefore, to understand the

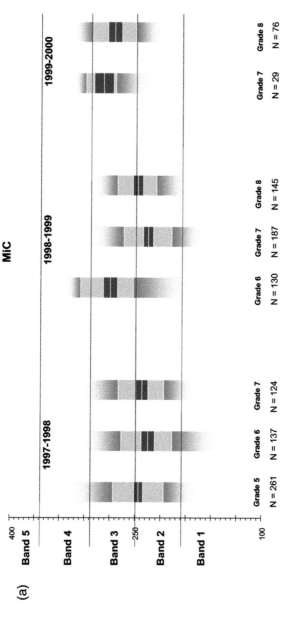

Figure 9.2a Distribution of classroom achievement in Grades 5, 6, and 7 in 1997–1998; Grades 6, 7, and 8 in 1998–1999; and Grades 7 and 8 in 1999–2000 in (a) the MiC treatment group, (b) the MiC (Conventional) treatment group, and (c) (overleaf) the Conventional treatment group.

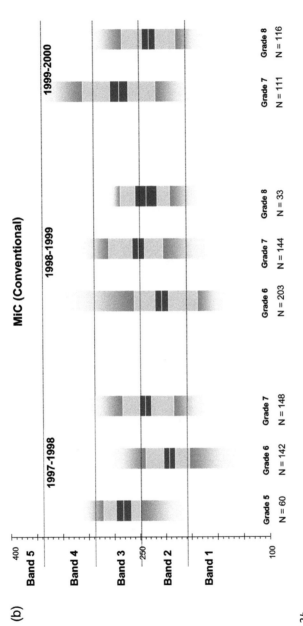

Figure 9.2b

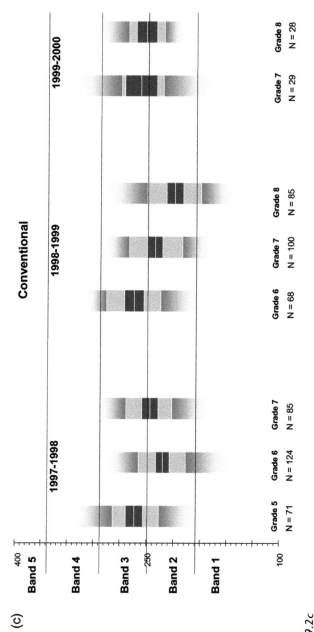

Figure 9.2c

differences in performance, it was important to examine critical differences in instruction and opportunity to learn with understanding among the teacher/student groups as well as differences in teachers' perceptions of school capacity.

In summary, although there was considerable variation in CA scores in the eight grade-level-by-year studies, the performance of the MiC treatment group tended to be higher than, or similar to, the performance of the Conventional treatment group, and both were often significantly higher than the MiC (Conventional) treatment group. However, when differences in overall means were found, these differences were best attributed to differences in teacher/student groups, and not simply to differences among the treatments.

Cross-grade studies

For the cross-grade studies, CA scores were aggregated to make comparisons of the performance of different groups of students at different grade levels. The usual underlying assumption of comparability in these studies is twofold: performance will likely increase over the grades and comparison of different groups of students at consecutive grade levels is possible because of the same social culture and schooling practice in a district. As noted in Chapter 8, however, we found both of these notions to be questionable. Comparability was constrained by homogeneous grouping, the shifting of (usually) students with higher prior achievement to district Grade 8 algebra initiatives, and the high attrition levels of both teachers and students.

Cross-grade comparisons in 1997–1998

For 1997–1998, performance on CA was aggregated for the three treatment groups in Grades 5, 6, and 7. (It is important to note that in District 2 a MiC (Conventional) treatment group was not available in Grade 5.) In four of the nine contrasts, the mean performances were significant (see Figure 9.3). In Grade 5, the mean scores of MiC (Conventional) and Conventional treatment groups were significantly higher than the MiC group. This difference in performance was consistent with the difference in prior achievement at this grade level. In Grade 6, the means for MiC and Conventional groups were significantly higher than the MiC (Conventional) group.

The Grade 5 scores for all three treatment groups were higher than the Grade 6 scores. However, this was due to the CA performance of teacher/student groups in District 1. The quality of instruction in MiC and some Conventional teacher/student groups was higher in Grade 5 than in Grade 6. Grade 5 teachers tended to teach for understanding, and students

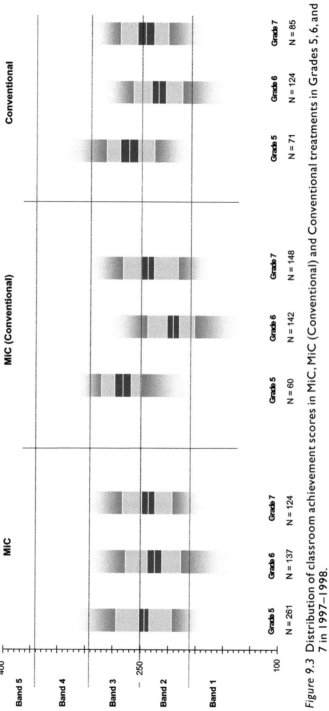

Figure 9.3 Distribution of classroom achievement scores in MiC, MiC (Conventional) and Conventional treatments in Grades 5, 6, and 7 in 1997–1998.

participated more fully in lessons and worked more collaboratively in small groups. In contrast, lessons for Grade 6 MiC (Conventional) and Conventional groups were underdeveloped or focused on procedures. Also, Grade 5 MiC and MiC (Conventional) teachers taught at least six MiC units that included content in all four strands, and they rarely supplemented MiC units with other resources. In comparison, Grade 6 MiC (Conventional) teachers taught fewer units, and the units were treated in ways that did not promote connections among mathematical ideas. Grade 6 Conventional teachers supplemented their textbooks with other resources, and content included primarily number. In District 1, the dip in performance in Grade 6 rebounded in Grade 7, but not to the level of Grade 5 performance. Thus, differences in overall student performance were attributable to differences in the teacher/student groups, not just differences in the three treatment groups.

Cross-grade comparisons in 1998–1999

For 1998–1999, performance on CA was aggregated for the three treatment groups in Grades 6, 7, and 8. (It is important to note that a MiC (Conventional) treatment group was not available in District 2 in Grade 8.) The MiC treatment group was the only group whose scores increased from Grade 7 to Grade 8, and the performance of the Conventional group was significantly lower from one grade level to another (see Figure 9.4). In four of the nine contrasts the mean performances were significant. The mean score of the MiC treatment group in Grade 6 was significantly higher than the MiC (Conventional) group in Grade 6 and the Conventional group in Grade 8. Also, in Grade 6 the mean performance of the Conventional group was higher than the MiC (Conventional) group. In Grade 7, the mean score of the MiC (Conventional) group was higher than the MiC group.

When the CA scores were reviewed by district, the four comparisons that were significant favored the MiC treatment group: in Grade 6 in District 1 the mean performance of the MiC treatment group was significantly higher than the other two groups; in Grade 6 in District 2 the mean of the MiC group was significantly higher than the MiC (Conventional) group; and in Grade 8 in District 2 the mean for the MiC group was significantly higher than the Conventional group. Examining these differences further, MiC teacher/student groups tended to teach for conceptual understanding, taught content from multiple content strands, and modified MiC units to a small degree. In contrast, teachers in MiC (Conventional) groups focused lessons on procedures or presented underdeveloped lessons, and supplemented MiC with skill practice. Therefore, the differences in overall student performance were attributable to differences in the teacher/student groups, not just differences in the three treatment groups.

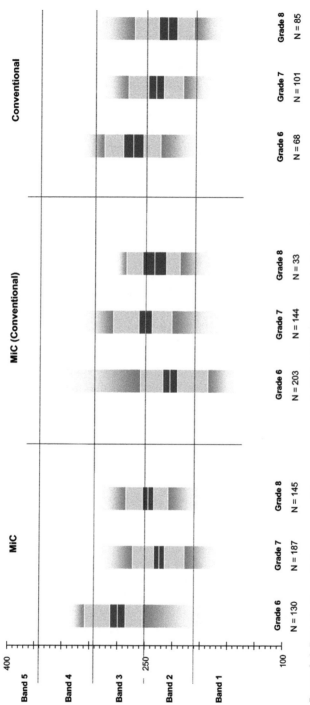

Figure 9.4 Distribution of classroom achievement scores in MiC, MiC (Conventional) and Conventional treatments in Grades 6, 7, and 8 in 1998–1999.

Cross-grade comparisons in 1999–2000

For 1999–2000, performance on CA was aggregated for the three treatment groups in Grades 7 and 8. (It is important to note that there was no MiC treatment group in Grade 7 in District 1, nor was there a Conventional group in Grade 8 in District 1.) In two of the six contrasts, mean performances were significant, and both favored the MiC treatment group (see Figure 9.5). The mean score for the MiC group in Grade 7 was higher than the Conventional group, and the mean for MiC group in Grade 8 was higher than the MiC (Conventional) group. By district, two of the three significant differences (in Grades 7 and 8 in District 2) favored the MiC treatment group over MiC (Conventional). In Grade 7 in District 1, the mean score for the MiC (Conventional) group was higher than the Conventional group. Again, differences in overall performance were attributable to differences in teacher/student groups.

In summary, cross-grade/cross-sectional comparisons involve different groups of students at different grade levels in the same districts. The assumption is that the groups of students will be comparable because they reflect the same social culture and schooling practices. Given this assumption, one expects to see increased performance over the grades on CA. This was not the case in our studies. The comparability of the three treatment groups was questionable. Nevertheless, the results show that although each treatment group outperformed the other groups in particular studies, most of the contrasts favored the MiC treatment group over both the MiC (Conventional) and Conventional groups, and the Conventional students sometimes outperformed the MiC (Conventional) students. Also, the differences in student performance were often attributable to differences in teacher/student groups, rather than solely differences in the three treatment groups.

Cross-year studies

Cross-year studies compare the results of students at the same grade level in the same district after studying MiC over two or three years. The assumptions are that students at a given grade level in the same district would be comparable and that the results might generate some insights into the performance of the same group of students as they studied a particular curriculum over time.

Grade 6 across two years

In both 1997–1998 (Year 1) and 1998–1999 (Year 2), CA data were aggregated for students at Grade 6. Overall, the mean CA scores for the MiC and Conventional treatment groups were significantly different over time (see Figure 9.6). However, more students in the MiC group were in Bands

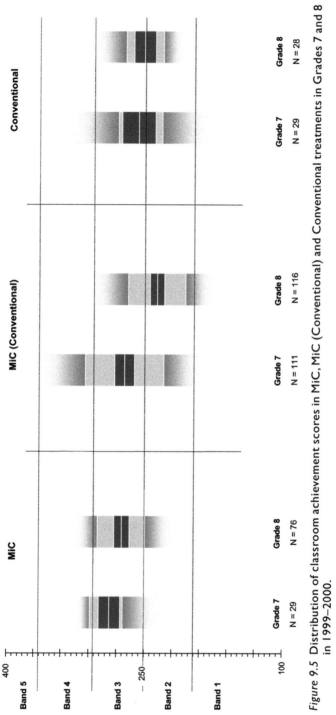

Figure 9.5 Distribution of classroom achievement scores in MiC, MiC (Conventional) and Conventional treatments in Grades 7 and 8 in 1999–2000.

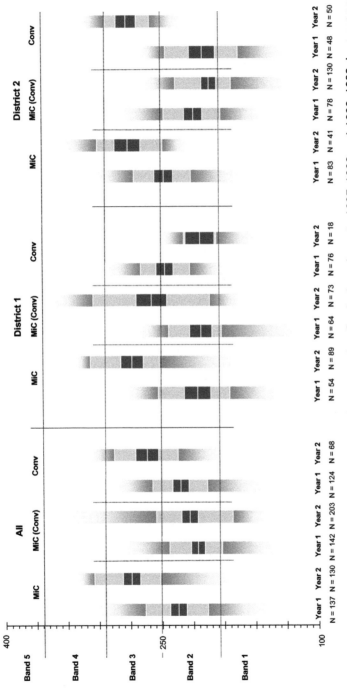

Figure 9.6 Cross-year comparisons of classroom achievement for Grade 6 students in 1997–1998 and 1998–1999, by treatment group, overall and by district.

3 and 4 than students in the Conventional group. Furthermore, the means for the MiC and Conventional treatment groups were significantly higher than the MiC (Conventional) group in both years.

In reviewing the scores by district, there were five instances in which the MiC treatment group significantly outperformed the MiC (Conventional) group and two instances in which they outperformed the Conventional group. There were also four cases that favored the Conventional group, one significantly higher than MiC and three higher than MiC (Conventional). These results reflect the differences in treatment groups found in the cross-grade studies. It should be noted that students in District 2 were different over time, as students in another middle school were added in Year 2 after teachers in one middle school withdrew from the study in Year 1.

Grade 7 across three years

For Years 1, 2, and 3 (1999–2000), CA data were aggregated for the three treatment groups at Grade 7. Overall, there were two significant differences between the groups (see Figure 9.7). In Year 2, the MiC (Conventional) group scored higher than the MiC group, and in Year 3, the MiC group scored higher than Conventional group.

In District 1, only one significant difference was evident, and that favored the MiC (Conventional) group over the Conventional group in Year 3. (A MiC treatment group was not available that year in District 1.) In District 2, there were four significant differences. In Year 2, the MiC and MiC (Conventional) groups outperformed the Conventional group. In Year 3, the MiC and Conventional groups outperformed the MiC (Conventional) group.

Grade 8 across two years

In Years 2 and 3, CA data were aggregated for the three treatment groups in Grade 8. Overall, in Year 2 the mean performance for the MiC treatment group was significantly higher than the Conventional group, and in Year 3 the mean for the MiC group was higher than the MiC (Conventional) group (see Figure 9.8). These differences were due to differences in scores in District 2, in which there was no MiC (Conventional) group in Year 2 and no Conventional group in Year 3.

In summary, cross-year comparisons involve different groups of students at the same grade levels in the same districts over two or three different years. The assumption is that the groups of students at a grade level will be comparable because they reflect the same social culture and schooling practices. In particular, because both teachers and students would be more familiar with MiC materials and instructional approach,

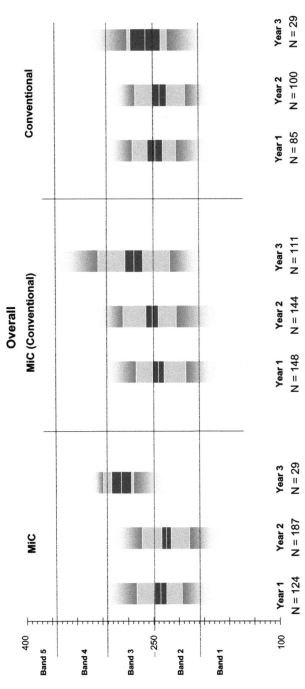

Figure 9.7 Cross-year comparisons of classroom achievement for Grade 7 students in 1997–1998, 1998–1999, and 1999–2000 by treatment group, overall and by district. (*Continued overleaf*)

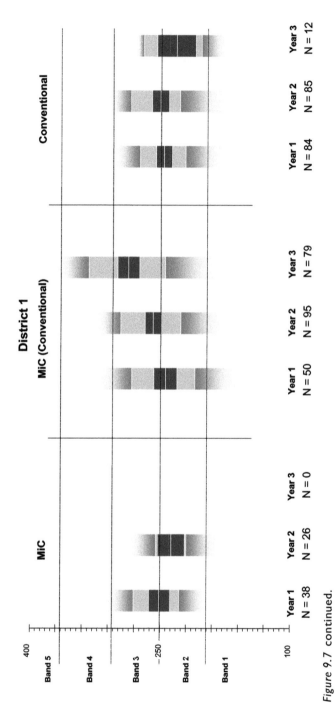

Figure 9.7 continued.

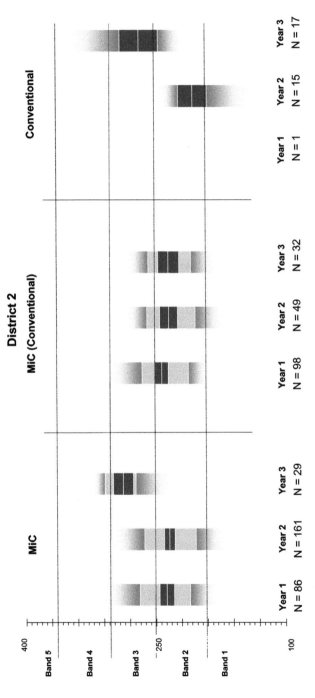

Figure 9.7 continued.

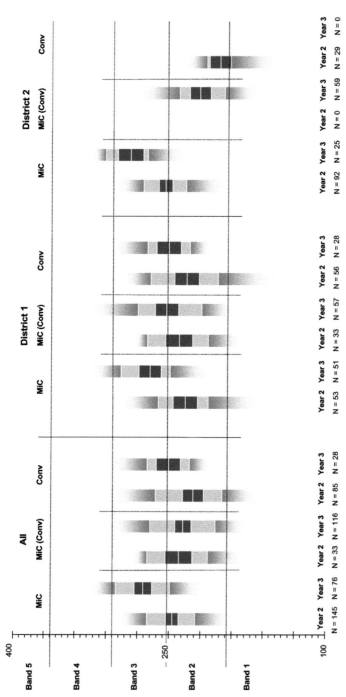

Figure 9.8 Cross-year comparisons of classroom achievement for Grade 8 students in 1998–1999 and 1999–2000 by treatment group, overall and by district.

one would expect to see increased CA performance over the years for MiC students. This expectation was supported in these three studies, particularly in the third year at Grade 7. In fact, for most of the significant contrasts, the MiC treatment group outperformed both of the other groups. The data also point to the importance of implementing MiC as intended because the MiC (Conventional) treatment group rarely performed differently than, and sometimes not as well as, the Conventional group. Also, there was ample evidence that in these districts there was increased performance by the MiC treatment group over time.

Longitudinal studies

The longitudinal studies carried out in order to answer Question 2 involved examining the CA performance of individual students who participated in the study for two or three years. This analysis involved only two treatment groups, MiC and Conventional, because the sample sizes of the MiC and MiC (Conventional) treatments were small.

The assumption underlying longitudinal research designs is that it is possible to track the growth in performance for individual students. Initially, longitudinal comparisons were planned for three cohorts of students, students who began in Grades 5, 6, and 7 in 1997–1998 (Cohorts A, B, and C, respectively). However, the number of students in these cohorts was small, which is attributable to several factors: dispersion of Grade 5 students as they entered middle school; lack of completion of both study assessments each year; withdrawn participation by four District 2 middle-school teachers; district mobility rates and parent school choice; and initiatives for students to take algebra in Grade 8. Four other cohorts were studied as well. Cohorts F and G included students who began their participation in 1997–1998 in Grades 5 and 6, respectively, and were followed for two years. Cohorts D and E included students who entered the study in 1998–1999 in Grades 6 and 7, respectively, and were followed for two years. (See Figure 9.9 for a summary of the cohorts studied in the longitudinal comparisons.)

CA scores were determined for students who completed both study assessments, the Problem Solving Assessment (PSA) and the External Assessment System (EAS), in each year of participation. Because student responses on assessment items were integral to the design of the proficiency scale for CA, missing scores were not statistically imputed. CA scores were aggregated for each of the seven cohort groups. However, the number of students for whom tests scores for each year were available was very small, particularly for Conventional students. Therefore, we also report five two-year contrasts that included students in combined cohorts AF (Grades 5 and 6), AD (Grades 6 and 7), BG (Grades 6 and 7), BE (Grades 7 and 8), and C (Grades 7 and 8).

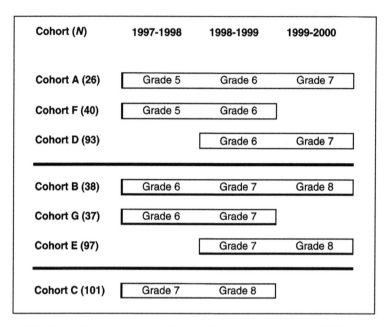

Figure 9.9 The cohorts studied in longitudinal comparisons of MiC and Conventional students.

Cohorts A, F, and AF

Cohort A began the study in 1997–1998, and they completed both study assessments in Grades 5, 6, and 7. This cohort was composed of 21 MiC students and 5 Conventional students. Cohort F also began the study in 1997–1998, but completed study assessments only in Grades 5 and 6. This cohort included 31 MiC students and 9 Conventional students. In each cohort, no significant differences in performance on CA were found for either treatment. Although the gain in CA performance for MiC students in Cohort A was only 6 points over the three years, the growth from Grade 6 to Grade 7—a gain of nearly 19 points—occurred after a 12.5-point decline in performance from Grade 5 to Grade 6. This is consistent with the findings in the grade-level-by-year studies. The means for MiC students in Cohort F decreased 6 points over the two years, which is consistent with the performance of Cohort A over the same two years. Unfortunately, the number of Conventional students in either cohort was too small to make meaningful comparisons.

In the combined Cohort AF, no significant differences in CA performance were found for MiC or Conventional students over the two years (see Figure 9.10). The mean of MiC students in Cohort AF declined 9

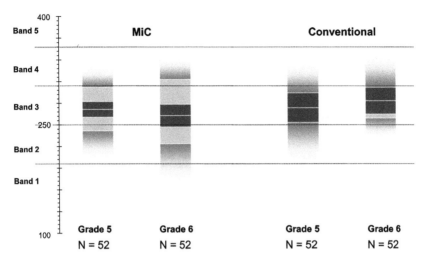

Figure 9.10 Distribution of classroom achievement scores for MiC and Conventional students in combined Cohort AF.

points, while the mean of Conventional students in Cohort AF increased 10 points over the two years.[1]

Cohorts A, D, and AD

In this analysis, we reviewed data for Cohort A only from Grades 6 and 7, which included 21 MiC students and 5 Conventional students. Cohort D students were new to the study in 1998–1999, and they completed both study assessments in Grades 6 and 7. This cohort included 85 MiC students and 8 Conventional students. The growth in CA performance for MiC students in both cohorts was substantial, nearly 20 points for each cohort. The number of conventional students in these cohorts was too small to make meaningful comparisons.

In the combined Cohort AD, no significant differences in CA performance were found for MiC or Conventional students over the two years (see Figure 9.11). However, the means for MiC students substantially increased nearly 20 points, while the means for Conventional students decreased 8 points.[2]

1 Three students were added in the Conventional group because CA data were available for them only in Grades 5 and 6.
2 Three students were added in the MiC and Conventional groups because CA data were available for them only in Grades 6 and 7.

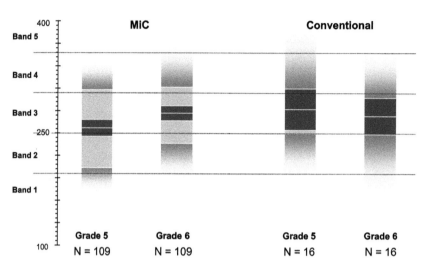

Figure 9.11 Distribution of classroom achievement scores for MiC and Conventional students in combined Cohort AD.

Cohorts B, G, and BG

Cohort B began the study in 1997–1998, and they completed both study assessments in Grades 6, 7, and 8. This cohort was composed of 36 MiC students and 2 Conventional students. Cohort G also began the study in 1997–1998, but completed study assessments only in Grades 6 and 7. This cohort included 24 MiC students and 13 Conventional students. The CA performance of MiC students in Cohort B rose significantly, 20 points over the three years. However, most of that increase occurred from Grade 6 to Grade 7. One might expect to see substantial increases from Grade 7 to Grade 8 as well. MiC students in Cohort G also showed substantial growth of nearly 23 points, while the means for Conventional students declined 20 points.

In the combined Cohort BG, the mean CA score for Conventional students in Grade 6 was significantly higher than for MiC students (see Figure 9.12). However, in Grade 7, the mean performance of MiC students showed a significant improvement of 31 points, while the mean for Conventional students dropped 13 points.

Cohorts B, E, and BE

In this analysis, we reviewed data for Cohort B only from Grades 7 and 8, which included 36 MiC students and 2 Conventional students. Cohort E students were new to the study in 1998–1999, and they completed both study assessments in Grades 7 and 8. This cohort included 73 MiC students

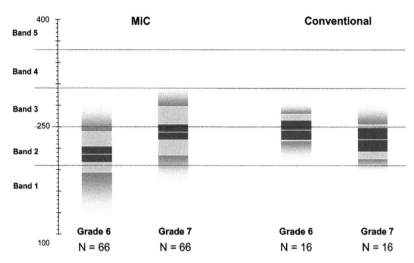

Figure 9.12 Distribution of classroom achievement scores for MiC and Conventional students in combined Cohort BG.

and 24 Conventional students. In both Cohorts B and E, MiC students showed minimal gain in CA scores over Grades 7 and 8 (4 points and 1 point, respectively). There were too few Conventional students in Cohort B to make any reasonable comparisons. However, Conventional students in Cohort E showed a decline of nearly 14 points from Grade 7 to Grade 8.

In the combined Cohort BE, no significant differences in CA performance were found for MiC or Conventional students over the two years (see Figure 9.13). The mean for the MiC students increased slightly (2 points), while the mean for Conventional students decreased 18 points.[3]

Cohort C

Cohort C included students who began the study in Grade 7 in 1997–1998 and completed both study assessments in Grades 7 and 8. This cohort consisted of 67 MiC students and 34 Conventional students. CA performance for MiC students increased 7 points, while the means for Conventional students declined 10 points (see Figure 9.14). However, in Grade 8, the mean for MiC students was significantly higher than the mean for Conventional students.

3 Twenty-eight students were added in the MiC group and three were added in the Conventional group because CA data were available for them only in Grades 7 and 8.

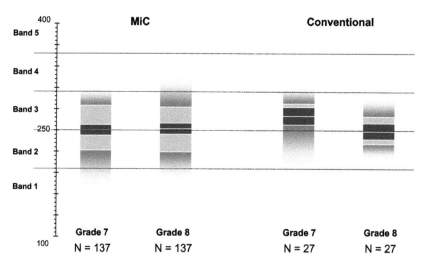

Figure 9.13 Distribution of classroom achievement scores for MiC and Conventional students in combined Cohort BE.

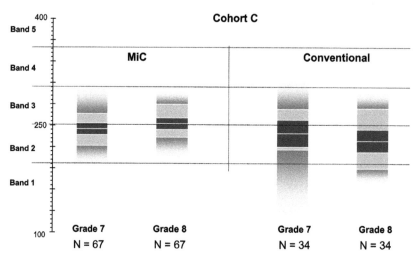

Figure 9.14 Distribution of classroom achievement scores for MiC and Conventional students in Cohort C.

In summary, we anticipated that the longitudinal contrasts would be critical in answering Question 2. Unfortunately, the small sample sizes over the three years of the study (and over two years for combined cohorts) seriously constrained meaningful comparisons. Nevertheless, in the contrasts between MiC and Conventional students who participated in the study for two years, there was one significant difference in achievement that favored MiC students (Cohort C in Grade 8). Also, in four of the five two-year cohort groups, scores of the MiC students increased over the two years, in contrast to declining scores of the Conventional students in four cases.

Two findings were surprising to us. In MiC cohorts beginning in Grade 5, performance declined from Grade 5 to Grade 6 and rebounded from Grade 6 to Grade 7. One would expect that students who studied the Grade 5 MiC units would be more successful in Grade 6. Second, in the three-year MiC cohort beginning in Grade 6, performance increased substantially from Grade 6 to Grade 7 but minimally from Grade 7 to Grade 8. One would expect to see substantial increases from Grade 7 to Grade 8 as well. These findings imply that differences in achievement involved more than the curriculum itself. Contributing factors such as instruction, opportunity to learn with understanding, and teachers' perceptions of school capacity are important in understanding changes in student performance.

The impact of prior achievement

The findings reported in this chapter suggest that the treatment groups differed on four key variables: student prior achievement, method of instruction, opportunity to learn with understanding (OTLu), and school capacity. As measures of prior achievement (PA), the research team used national percentile rankings from the regularly scheduled standardized testing programs in each district: *TerraNova* (CTB/McGraw-Hill, 1997) in District 1 and *Stanford Mathematics Achievement Test* (Harcourt Brace Educational Measurement, 1997) in District 2. Instruction, OTLu, and school capacity were scaled on the composite index created for each. We examined the overall impact of these four variables on CA scores through analysis of variance using a SAS program (SAS Institute, 2000). Although the overall impact of these variables on CA was significant, only a third of the variance was attributable to these variables. When we examined the separate contribution of the four variables, the impact of only one variable was significant, PA. This finding was surprising because differences in instruction and OTLu led us to identify three distinct treatment groups. When we explored the correlations between the variables, we found that CA and PA means were strongly correlated, instruction and OTLu were significantly correlated with CA, and school capacity was weakly correlated with CA. Furthermore, instruction and OTLu were strongly correlated. These results validated our use of the differences in these variables in determining the three treatment groups.

Because PA contributed the most to CA scores, we looked at the overall CA and PA means for the three treatment groups. We found that the CA and PA means were higher for the MiC treatment group than the MiC

(Conventional) group and the Conventional group, which had the lowest mean. Therefore, we used PA scores as a covariate in order to adjust the CA means to account for these differences. As a result, the differences in the means for each treatment were reduced, while the order of the means remained the same. This finding justified our use of PA as a covariate in subsequent analyses.

Analysis of covariance

The overall differences in mean achievement for the three treatment groups are reported here for all years and grade levels with teacher/student group as the unit of analysis. Using CA as the dependent variable for groups at different grades in different years is possible because we were able to calibrate a single proficiency scale that incorporated items from all assessments. Finally, because a priori the groups differed on several measures, the statistical model used for this analysis was analysis of covariance (ANCOVA) with prior achievement (PA) as the covariate. The means and adjusted means for the three groups are shown in Table 9.5.

The overall difference in CA means significantly favored the MiC group over the Conventional group (Romberg, Shafer, Folgert, & LeMire, 2005). When initial differences in achievement were taken into account, the overall performance of MiC and MiC (Conventional) groups were different with a moderate effect size, and the performance of MiC (Conventional) and Conventional groups were similar. We then compared the performance of the treatment groups on each study assessment independently. The results on both assessments were similar to the CA findings. The MiC treatment group significantly outperformed the Conventional group with a substantial effect size, and the MiC group outperformed the MiC (Conventional) group with a moderate effect size. No differences in the performances of the MiC (Conventional) and Conventional groups were found on either assessment.

We found similar results when we reviewed students' achievement on the Problem Solving Assessments (PSA) by content strand. In algebra, geometry, and statistics, the MiC treatment group scored significantly higher

Table 9.5 Classroom achievement, prior achievement, and least squares means for the three treatment groups

Treatment	Teacher/ student groups (N)	CA Mean	Std Deviation	PA Mean	Std Deviation	Least squares mean
MiC	28	254.53	27.71	52.21	16.50	252.01
MiC (Conventional)	28	241.98	27.85	47.76	15.09	243.89
Conventional	23	236.45	31.36	48.92	19.39	237.20

than the Conventional group with substantial effect sizes. In number, the MiC group scored higher (but not significantly higher) than the other treatment groups with a moderate effect size in each case. This result is contrary to the voiced intent of many MiC (Conventional) teachers who deliberately augmented the MiC materials with conventional materials on number because they believed that MiC was weak on number. On the geometry scale, the MiC group's achievement was significantly higher than that of the Conventional group. Again, this is consistent with the differences in content coverage between MiC and conventional materials. However, the MiC level of achievement was similar to that of the MiC (Conventional) group in geometry. This implies that many of the MiC (Conventional) teachers taught some of the MiC geometry units.

To illustrate these differences we have chosen to examine the differences between the three groups on the algebra scale. The raw means and the adjusted means for the algebra scale are shown in Table 9.6.

There was a significant difference between MiC and Conventional groups with a substantial effect size and effect size correlation. There was a moderate effect size difference between the MiC and MiC (Conventional) groups, but there were no differences between the MiC (Conventional) and Conventional groups on the algebra scale.

The following pair of items from the Grade 6 PSA illustrates the basis of the differences in algebra between the three groups. The first item assesses students' abilities to use a formula, calculate (multiply and subtract) with whole and decimal numbers, use order of operations, provide a correct answer, and show appropriate work (see Figure 9.15).

The second item assesses students' abilities to solve for the unknown in a given formula, calculate (subtract and divide) with whole and decimal numbers, and provide a correct answer with clear supporting work (see Figure 9.16).

The scoring guides for these items allow for 0, 1, or 2 points depending on both answer and work. The difference in means for the three groups on these items is given in Table 9.7.

Our primary conclusion about the differences between the three treatment groups is that the overall achievement for the MiC teacher/student

Table 9.6 Algebra scale means and adjusted means for the three treatment groups

Treatment	Teacher/student groups (N)	Algebra scale mean	Least squares mean
MiC	28	255.88	254.05
MiC (Conventional)	28	244.31	245.53
Conventional	23	239.59	240.33

Birds lose weight when they fly. For example, a swan loses about 01.1 kilograms of weight for each hour flying.

When you know the weight of a swan at the beginning of a flight—the starting weight in kilograms—you can compute the landing weight with the following formula:

landing weight = starting weight – N × 0.1

In this formula the landing weight is the weight in kilograms after a flight of **N** hours.

11. If a swan has a starting weight of 10.5 kilograms, how much will it weigh after flying 7 hours? Show your work.

Figure 9.15 Item 11 from Grade 6 Problem Solving Assessment.

Birds lose weight when they fly. For example, a swan loses about 01.1 kilograms of weight for each hour flying.

When you know the weight of a swan at the beginning of a flight—the starting weight in kilograms—you can compute the landing weight with the following formula:

landing weight = starting weight – N × 0.1

In this formula the landing weight is the weight in kilograms after a flight of **N** hours.

A swan weighed 13 kilograms. After a flight its weight dropped to 11.9 kilograms.

12. How many hours has this swan been flying? Show your work.

Figure 9.16 Item 12 from Grade 6 Problem Solving Assessment.

Table 9.7 Means of Grade 6 Problem Solving Assessment sample items 11 and 12 by treatment

		MiC		MiC (Conventional)		Conventional	
Item	Content strand(s)	(N)	Mean	(N)	Mean	(N)	Mean
#11	Algebra/Number	267	0.73	368	0.37	231	0.64
#12	Algebra/Number	267	0.56	368	0.21	231	0.38

groups was higher than the achievement of MiC (Conventional) or Conventional groups when differences for prior achievement that favored the MiC group were taken into account. Although this overall analysis masks the within-group variation due to differences in school districts, grade levels, or teachers in the different treatment groups, this finding implies that achievement will increase as students study a reform curriculum like MiC when it is implemented as intended. Regardless of other differences, when MiC was implemented as intended, students showed higher achievement than partial implementation of the curriculum and performed better than students who studied a conventional curriculum.

A final conclusion about the differences between the treatment groups is that it is difficult to distinguish the differences in achievement between the MiC (Conventional) and Conventional groups. With the exception of the differences in achievement on the geometry scale, the performances of these groups were very similar. The implication of this finding is that augmenting a reform curriculum with conventional materials or augmenting a conventional curriculum with reform materials is not likely to result in different student performance.

Summary

In these analyses of the differences between the three treatment groups, the overall achievement of the MiC treatment group was higher than the achievement of the MiC (Conventional) and Conventional groups when the differences in prior achievement that favored the MiC group were taken into account. This was also evident in the separate results of the External Assessment System and the Problem Solving Assessments. Thus, regardless of other differences in the teacher/student groups, when MiC was implemented as intended, students had higher achievement scores than students who experienced partial implementation of the curriculum and students who used a conventional curriculum. Furthermore, the achievement of the MiC group was higher than other groups in number on the Problem Solving Assessments. This finding is contrary to the actions of many MiC (Conventional) teachers who deliberately supplemented MiC with conventional skill-practice materials because they believed that MiC was weak in number. In algebra, geometry, and statistics, the achievement of the MiC group was significantly higher than the other groups. This is consistent with the differences in content coverage between MiC and conventional materials. Also, the achievement of the MiC group in geometry was similar to the MiC (Conventional) group. This implies that many of the MiC (Conventional) teachers taught some of the MiC geometry units. We also found that it was difficult to distinguish the differences in achievement between the MiC (Conventional) and Conventional groups. With the exception of the differences in geometry, the performances of these treatment groups were very similar. The implication of this finding is that supplementing a reform curriculum with conventional materials or teaching a reform curriculum with conventional pedagogy is not likely to result in different student performance.

Answer to Question 2

In various ways we investigated how student performance differed between that when using MiC and when using conventional materials. We found that the impact varied not only in students' prior achievement, but also in the ways teachers implemented their curricula. When the implementation of MiC was aligned with the philosophy of the curriculum, student achievement was significantly higher than when teachers nominally implemented the curriculum by using a combination of MiC with conventional materials or when they taught MiC with conventional methods. In fact, student achievement in the group with nominal implementation was similar to achievement of students who used conventional curricula. We illustrate these differences with Grade 8 teacher/student groups in 1999–2000 who began the school year with comparable prior achievement scores (CA scores from the prior school year). We contrast the implementation of curricula in the MiC group of Mr Gallardo, the MiC (Conventional) group of Ms Waters, and the Conventional group of Ms Wolfe. For each of these groups, the level of instruction that transpired during the school year and changes in students' performance are shown in Figure 9.17 (Shafer et al., 2005).

Mr Gallardo actively worked with his students to promote conceptual understanding. He effectively posed questions that encouraged students to explain their thinking, orchestrated substantive whole class discussions, and helped students make connections among mathematical ideas. Classroom interactions were used to promote making sense of the mathematics. By the end of Grade 8, the mean performance of Mr Gallardo's group jumped 37 points and was the highest gain among all teacher/student groups in Grade 8 that year. Mr Gallardo taught the same students in both Grades 7 and 8. The quality of instruction (Levels 4 and 5) and moderate to high OTLu (Levels 3 and 4) students experienced over time likely affected the significant gains in student performance.

Although Ms Waters wanted students to do the mathematical work required in MiC units, she tended to do the work for them by presenting strategies or procedures after small group work. Class discussions were not substantive. Students provided only answers to Ms Waters' questions or their explanations were about procedures, and multiple strategies were generally not elicited. Few questions promoted conceptual understanding, and connections were discussed infrequently. The instruction experienced by Ms Waters' group (Level 2) was more reflective of conventional pedagogy. Furthermore, although Ms Waters taught MiC throughout the school year, she emphasized number and algebra units (OTL*u* at Level 3). This combination of instruction and OTL*u* led to the classification of Ms Waters' group as MiC (Conventional). Implementing MiC with conventional pedagogy likely influenced the slight gain (4 points) in performance for these students.

Ms Wolfe presented particular procedures, and students practiced them in a rote fashion. Using a conventional textbook, mathematics content spanned a vast content plane with little or no depth, and inquiry

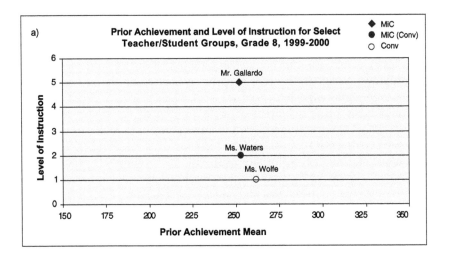

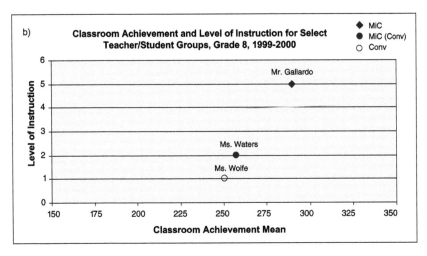

Figure 9.17 Comparison of (a) prior achievement and (b) classroom achievement for select teacher/student groups in Grade 8, 1999–2000, by level of instruction.

during instruction was limited to lower order thinking. Ms Wolfe's group experienced a low quality of instruction (Level 1) and OTL*u* (Level 1), which likely influenced the 11-point decline in CA performance this year.

In summary, students' prior achievement had an important impact on classroom achievement. However, the implementation of curricular materials also influenced changes in student achievement over time. The implementation of MiC by study teachers varied to the point that two treatment groups were distinguished among them. MiC teachers implemented the curriculum as intended, with an instructional philosophy of teaching mathematics for understanding and the use of MiC with few supplementary conventional materials. MiC (Conventional) teachers either nominally used MiC with extensive supplementary materials or taught MiC throughout the school year with conventional instructional methods. This variation in implementation led to distinctions in student performance. When differences in prior achievement that favored the MiC group were taken into account, and when teacher/student groups of comparable prior achievement were examined, classroom achievement for MiC teacher/student groups was significantly higher than MiC (Conventional) groups in overall performance and in number, algebra, and statistics, and the performance of MiC (Conventional) groups was often similar to the performance of Conventional groups. Thus, regardless of other differences in the teacher/student groups, when MiC was implemented as intended, students had higher achievement scores than students who experienced implementation that was less aligned with the philosophy of the curriculum and students who used conventional curricular materials.

Chapter 10

Findings about student achievement, question 3: what variables associated with classroom instruction account for variation in student performance?

The research model for our study included 14 variables in five categories—prior, independent, intervening, outcome, and consequent (see Figure 1.1 in Chapter 1). This model was used as the framework for data collection and analysis (see Romberg & Shafer, 2004). Initially, we planned to use structural equations to examine the relationship of the variables for the eight grade-level-by-year studies in classes using MiC across all four districts. In practice, this was not done because it was difficult or impossible to gather reliable information on all variables, the sample size was compromised over time, and collinearity across some variables posed a serious interpretation problem. Thus, a simplified model was designed using composite variables that we were able to scale.

As pointed out in Chapter 1, the simplified research model posits that variations in classroom achievement (CA) can be attributed to variations in prior achievement (PA), method of instruction (I), opportunity to learn with understanding (OTLu), and the capacity of schools to support mathematics teaching and learning (SC). This relationship can be expressed as—

$$CA = PA + I + OTL\,u + SC$$

In this chapter, we describe the relationship between the composite variables and the initial model, summarize the impact of these variables on student performance, and explain reasons that we were unable to gather data on other variables in the initial model.

Outcome and consequent variables

Three outcome variables were included in the structural model: *Knowledge and Understanding, Application*, and *Attitudes*. The instruments we developed to measure the outcome variables were described in Chapter 7. The External Assessment System (EAS) was designed to measure the variable *Knowledge and Understanding*. Each of the four grade-level assessments contained mostly multiple-choice items from publicly released tasks from the NAEP and TIMSS, which were evenly divided among four strands: number, geometry, algebra, and statistics and probability. Five items in each content strand, referred to as anchor items, were used on each grade level assessment to monitor growth in student achievement over time. The Problem Solving Assessments System (PSA) was designed to measure the variable *Application*. The PSAs were designed to align with the general reform curricular goals of problem solving, communication, reasoning, and connections. All items were constructed response, and students were explicitly asked to demonstrate how they determined their answers. The four content strands were addressed on each assessment.

Data from the EAS and PSA assessments were used to create the composite index for classroom achievement (CA) in the simplified research model (see Turner & O'Connor, 2005). This composite index was used as the measure of student performance in the study.[1] As described in Chapters 8 and 9, it is clear from analysis of CA in the eight grade-level-by-year studies that there was considerable variability in the CA scores whether examining overall performance (see Table 10.1 and Figure 10.1), performance by district, or performance by teacher/student groups (Romberg et al., 2005b). There was similar variability in the separate indices created for the EAS and the PSA. However, although both sets of assessments contributed to the six achievement bands of the CA index, the EAS items tended to contribute to the lower achievement bands and the PSA items to the higher achievement bands (Turner & O'Connor, 2005).

The third outcome variable was *Attitudes* toward mathematics. We gathered attitude information each year through the Student Attitude Inventory we created for the study (Shafer et al., 1997b). This instrument gathered information on seven subscales: effort to succeed in mathematics, interest in and excitement about mathematics, confidence in learning mathematics, communication of mathematical ideas, usefulness of mathematics, general perceptions about mathematics and learners of mathematics, and attribution of success or failure in mathematics. We wanted to see whether students' experiences learning mathematics with a more comprehensive and engaging curriculum would improve their attitudes toward mathematics.

---

1 Depending on the analysis, the CA scores were disaggregated to report performance scores for EAS, PSA, the four content strands, and the EAS anchor items. CA gain scores were also calculated. Additionally, districts provided student standardized test scores each year, which we used as another measure of the variable *Knowledge and Understanding*. Finally, for the students in the longitudinal comparisons an assessment of mathematical reasoning was used as another measure of performance.

Table 10.1 Overall MiC classroom achievement for the eight grade-level-by-year studies

	(N)	Mean	SD	95% Confidence interval		Score distribution percentiles			
				Lower	Upper	95%tile	75%tile	25%tile	5%tile
Grade 5, Year 1	448	255.2	43.7	251.1	259.2	330.7	281.6	228.5	185.0
Grade 6, Year 1	503	239.9	48.9	235.7	244.2	316.6	275.9	206.5	165.2
Grade 7, Year 1	507	252.8	49.2	248.5	257.1	326.2	285.0	221.7	170.3
Grade 6, Year 2	550	249.4	56.4	244.7	254.1	338.0	294.6	209.8	163.0
Grade 7, Year 2	636	248.8	44.9	245.3	252.3	321.1	278.7	216.1	180.5
Grade 8, Year 2	319	249.0	45.9	244.0	254.0	321.9	279.9	219.4	179.3
Grade 7, Year 3	267	282.2	52.2	276.0	288.5	360.6	316.6	246.8	188.9
Grade 8, Year 3	255	251.9	42.7	246.7	252.7	319.4	282.7	219.4	189.5

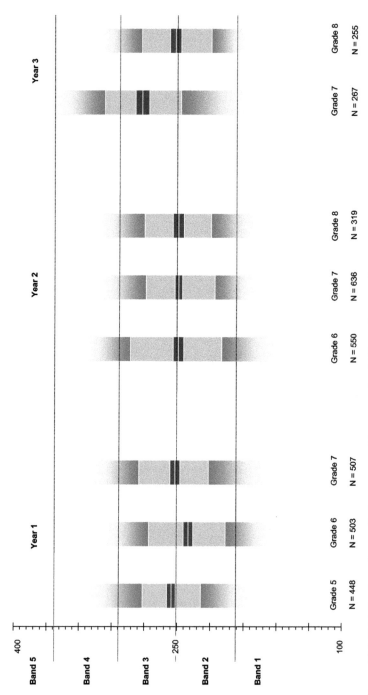

Figure 10.1 Distribution of overall classroom achievement for MiC students in the eight grade-level-by-year studies.

Although we gathered attitude data each year, we did not attempt to develop a single composite variable for it and did not include it in the simplified research model. Our decision not to use student attitudes as a dependent variable was based on two findings. First, in our examination of the data gathered at the beginning of the study, we found very little variability (Romberg & Shafer, 2004a). Attitudes were uniformly high for all students, indicating little possibility for growth. Second, across the various categories of data we were unable to identify any discernable pattern, which was essential for developing a single composite scale.

At the beginning of the study, there were no real differences between students who studied MiC and students who studied conventional curricula on the first five subscales. However, on the general perception subscale, there were three significant differences. The MiC group agreed more strongly that it was okay to solve mathematics problems differently than classmates, and they disagreed more strongly that they would get a correct answer if they used a memorized rule or fact. In addition, the Conventional group agreed more strongly that they were able to learn new ideas in mathematics class. For these six subscales in all teacher/student groups, the results were similar and very positive, and the standard deviations were minimal. With respect to attribution of success and failure, students strongly attributed both success and failure to effort, not to their teachers or luck. The only significant difference was that students who studied conventional curricula were more convinced that ability does not contribute to failure.

One consequent variable, *Further Pursuits*, was included in the structural research model. As students begin Grade 9, they undoubtedly have expectations (and perhaps reservations) about their future success in mathematics courses. The transition into high-school mathematics as well as the number and type of courses they intend to take in high school are affected by the extent of success they had during their middle-school years. As students learn broader mathematics content with greater involvement in their learning, we expect students will continue to study mathematics, exceeding the minimum requirements for high-school graduation.

To measure *Further Pursuits*, we developed an additional student questionnaire (Shafer, 1999) using items that examined students' transition from primary to secondary schools (Clarke, 1989). We collected data about the nature of students' experiences in both middle-school and high-school mathematics classes; the types of mathematics courses students intended to study in high school; and students' conceptions about learning mathematics. In January 2000 the questionnaire was sent to 9th-grade students who had participated in the study as 7th- and 8th-grade students. Student questionnaires were distributed by counselors in the high schools attended by study participants in Districts 1–3. (Questionnaires were not sent to students in District 4 because of the dispersion of study students in numerous high schools in the district.) Students were asked to complete the questionnaires under the supervision of their parents and return the questionnaires to the research center in postage-paid envelopes. Unfortunately, the response rate was very low, and we were unable to draw any conclusions about this variable. Consequently, the questionnaires were not distributed to other students the following year.

Prior variables

In the structural research model, the prior variables included *Student Background*, the *Social Context* or culture in which a particular school operates, and *Teacher Background*. In the simplified model only the prior knowledge of students is considered, and it is represented as prior achievement (PA).

Student background

Not surprisingly, prior achievement in mathematics is a good predictor of achievement in subsequent years. For example, using CA scores for the group of all students[2] in Districts 1, 2, and 4[3] at the end of Grade 7 in 1999 as a measure of prior achievement (PA) and CA scores at the end of Grade 8 in 2000 as a measure of current achievement, the overall correlation of scores was 0.65, which indicates a strong relationship between PA and CA (see Table 10.2; Romberg et al., 2005b). By district, correlations for students in each district were 0.76, 0.56, and 0.60 for Districts 1, 2, and 4, respectively. Furthermore, a strong correlation (0.88) was evident when examining the means by teacher/student group. Within each district, the correlations of teacher/student groups were 0.99, 0.92, and 0.83 for Districts 1, 2, and 4, respectively. Thus, in all examined cases, strong correlations between PA and CA were evident.

To further investigate the correlation between PA and CA in 1997–1998, scatter plots of PA using the standardized test scores from the prior year and the CA scores in 1998 were constructed (Romberg et al., 2004). For example, the scatter plot for teacher/student groups in Grade 5 in District 1 showed a linear relationship between PA and CA means (see Figure 10.2). Entering Grade 5, the standardized test scores indicated that "high scoring" students were in Teacher 31's group, "average scoring" students were in the groups of Teachers 19 and 27, and "lower scoring" students were in the groups of Teachers 4, 14, and 49. The CA scores at the end of Grade 5

---

2   The students included in this analysis completed both study assessments in 1999 and 2000.

3   Data for Grade 8 students in District 3 were unavailable in 2000.

Table 10.2 Prior achievement and classroom achievement correlations for Grade 8 MiC students in 1999–2000, by district and teacher/student group

District and teacher/student group	(N)[1]	Spring 1999 classroom achievement score		Spring 2000 classroom achievement score		Correlation coefficient[2]	District correlation of mean[3]
		Mean	St Dev	Mean	St Dev		
District 1							0.99
75	23	258.71	48.30	263.05	47.24	0.78	
91	9	247.18	36.71	242.73	43.92	0.77	
87	36	263.81	39.19	272.88	40.00	0.73	
District 1 Students	68	259.88	41.95	265.56	43.59	0.76	
District 2							0.92
45	9	274.79	28.83	291.42	18.78	0.68	
62	10	259.15	43.68	282.98	36.67	0.64	
70	41	230.62	45.59	214.33	36.47	0.39	
95	10	233.00	36.29	246.84	33.13	0.63	
District 2 Students	70	240.71	44.63	238.69	46.26	0.56	
District 4							0.83
29	9	225.72	31.85	233.12	40.15	0.62	
66	26	249.07	24.89	271.79	29.71	0.50	
89	14	245.91	37.78	245.83	26.50	0.72	
District 4 Students	49	243.88	30.91	257.27	34.36	0.60	
District 1, 2, 4 Students	187	248.51	41.17	253.33	43.84	0.65	
Correlation of Class Means							0.88

[1] The N in this table represents all of the students with both Spring 1999 and Spring 2000 classroom achievement scores.
[2] These correlations are of student scores by teacher, district, and all districts.
[3] These correlations are between class means within and across all districts.

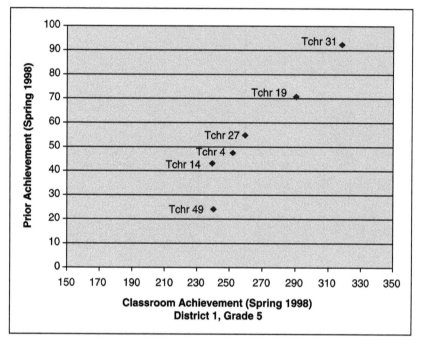

Figure 10.2 Scatter plot of prior achievement and classroom achievement of Grade 5 teacher/student groups in District 1, 1997–1998.

reflected the prior standardized test scores. Not only were the two sets of scores highly correlated, it was clear that students were grouped for instruction based on their prior performance, which was confirmed in principal and teacher interviews.

In Chapter 9, the results of another investigation of the relationship of PA to CA suggested that the PA means for the MiC, MiC (Conventional), and Conventional treatment groups varied, the mean PA score for the MiC group was higher than means of the other groups, and PA was significantly related to CA (Romberg et al., 2005a). Because of the strong relationship of PA to CA, it was important to use PA as a covariate and CA as the dependent variable in analysis of covariance (ANCOVA) when comparing treatment groups on CA. When the differences in PA that favored the MiC group were taken into account, CA for MiC teacher/student groups was significantly higher than MiC (Conventional) groups, and the performance of MiC (Conventional) groups was often similar to the performance of Conventional groups. Thus, when MiC was implemented as intended, students had higher CA scores than students who experienced implementation that was less aligned with the philosophy of the curriculum and students who used conventional curricular materials.

We also examined the effect of PA on student attitudes toward mathematics (Romberg et al., 2005). We found that PA did not contribute to the variance in any of the first five subscales (effort, interest, confidence, communication, and usefulness). However, PA contributed significantly to students' attitudes on only 2 of 16 statements in the general perceptions subscale: it is okay to solve mathematics problems differently than classmates and it is possible for students to solve problems in ways that others had not considered. Thus, although PA was strongly correlated with CA, PA generally did not contribute to differences in student attitudes over time.

Other student background information was gathered, including information on gender, ethnicity, and profiles of students' reasoning in mathematics (Romberg et al., 2004). The data for MiC students in Grade 6 in 1998–1999 illustrate the patterns of variation in performance by gender and ethnicity (see Figure 10.3). Males and females had very similar distributions of CA scores, and these scores reflected the same wide variance as the total population. However, the performances differed by ethnic group. Although the within group distributions showed the wide variance of performance for the overall student sample, in all eight grade-level-by-year studies, the performance of White students was higher than African–American students, and the performance of White students was similar to and higher than the performance of Hispanic students and Other[4] students, respectively.

We also gathered information on students' mathematical reasoning based on scores derived from the *Collis-Romberg Mathematical Problem Solving Profiles* (Collis & Romberg, 1992). The *Collis-Romberg Profiles* contained five mathematical problem-solving situations and four questions for each situation which were based on Biggs and Collis' (1982) SOLO taxonomy used to classify the structure of observed learning outcomes. Each question was designed to require more sophisticated use of the information from the stem in order to obtain a correct result. This increase in sophistication should parallel the increasing complexity of structure noted in the SOLO categories. Form A of the *Collis-Romberg Profiles* was used as a pre-test in Year 1. We found low levels of performance (generally at the uni-structural level, indicating the use of one obvious piece of information coming directly from the stem) and little variability. In the final spring of each student's participation in the study, Form B was administered as a post-test. When we examined the changes in the *Profiles* for the longitudinal cohort groups of MiC students, the results showed reasonable gains. For example, students in Cohort C (students who completed both

---

4 Other students included Asian students, Haitian students, Native American students, Multiracial students, and Other students.

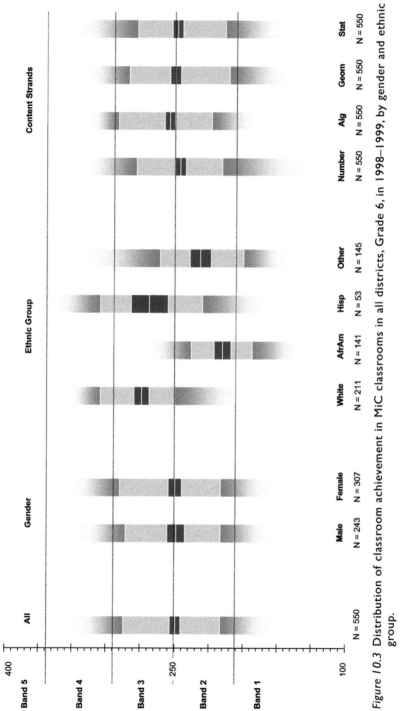

Figure 10.3 Distribution of classroom achievement in MiC classrooms in all districts, Grade 6, in 1998–1999, by gender and ethnic group.

the EAS and PSA in Grades 7 and 8 in 1998 and 1999) showed a reasonable shift in level of reasoning from Form A to Form B (see Table 10.3). There was a considerable reduction of percent at the uni-structural level with a corresponding increase in percent at the multi-structural level. However, we were surprised at the percent of the MiC students classified as pre-structural at the end of Grade 8. This implies that these students were unable to answer the majority of first questions for each stem. Similarly, the few students at the relational level at the end of the study is worrisome, for it is assumed that students should be at that level if they are to take a formal algebra course.

In summary, strong correlations between prior achievement and classroom achievement were evident in each of the eight grade-level-by-year studies for MiC students, and it was apparent that some students were grouped for instruction based on their prior performance. However, prior achievement generally did not contribute to differences in student attitudes over time. Males and females had very similar performances, but the performances of the ethnic groups differed, with White students performing higher than African–American students and similar to and higher than the performance of Hispanic students and Other students, respectively. Students' mathematical reasoning showed reasonable gains over time, although few students were at a level of reasoning deemed important for taking a formal algebra course at the end of Grade 8.

School context

The four districts in our study differed in location, percent of students in various ethnic groups, and socioeconomic status. For example, in 1998–1999, performance on CA was gathered for students in all districts at Grades 6, 7, and 8 (see Figure 10.4). Several things were of interest in these data (Romberg et al., 2005b). First, the overall CA means at each grade were almost identical. Second, in District 1 the means for each grade were significantly lower from one grade to another. Third, the means for each grade level in District 2 increased significantly over the three grade levels, and the means increased significantly from Grade 7 to Grade 8 in District 3. Finally, the pattern in District 4 was mixed (a significant increase from Grade 6 to Grade 7 and a significant decrease from Grades 6 and 7 to Grade 8). The lower scores for Grade 8 students in Year 3 reflected the shift of (usually) higher achieving students to an algebra class that year.

Similar profiles of student performance in the other two years of the study make it clear that school context affected student performance with students in District 3 outperforming students in other districts. However, district variation was confounded by variation in student ethnicity.

Table 10.3 Performance on the Collis-Romberg Mathematical Problem-Solving Profiles—Forms A and B for MiC students in Cohort C

Cohort C	(N)	Level of student performance					
		Prestructural	Unistructural	Multistructural	Relational	Extended Abstract	Not available
			Mathematics in Context				
CR-A	67	16	78	4	1	0	0
CR-B	67	13	49	34	0	0	3

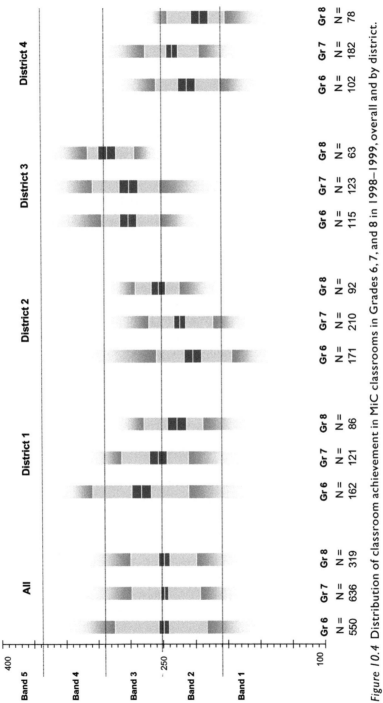

Figure 10.4 Distribution of classroom achievement in MiC classrooms in Grades 6, 7, and 8 in 1998–1999, overall and by district.

Teacher background

We gathered information about mathematics preparation, teaching experience, conceptions about mathematics teaching and learning, and use of assessment procedures from each study teacher. However, there were no discernable differences in the range of teaching experience and educational background in mathematics among study teachers, and most teachers had participated in recent professional development activities. Furthermore, all teachers expressed similar views about mathematics teaching and learning. Because the differences in teacher background were minimal, the information was not scaled for use in any further analyses.

Independent and intervening variables

In the structural research model, four independent variables, *Curricular Content and Materials*, the *Support Environment* available for students and teachers, *Teacher Knowledge*, and *Teacher Professional Responsibility*, and three intervening variables, *Pedagogical Decisions, Classroom Events*, and *Student Pursuits*, are represented. Using data from these variables, three composite variables were created, which were used in the simplified research model: instruction (I), opportunity to learn with understanding (OTL*u*), and school capacity (SC). In this section, we discuss the relationships between the composite variables and student achievement and between the independent and intervening variables and student achievement.

Instruction

The composite index for instruction emphasized key elements of instruction including pedagogical decisions, classroom events, and student pursuits (Shafer, 2005a). With respect to pedagogical decisions, seven aspects of planning were scaled that ranged from students' performance in previous lessons to planning lesson activities that promoted discussion, problem solving, and reflection on lesson content. We identified and scaled the on-the-spot decisions teachers made that affected learning of the mathematics. In addition, we scaled five aspects of classroom events, focusing on specific aspects such as the nature of inquiry and the nature of students' explanations, and three aspects of classroom assessment practice including the information teachers sought in assessing students' understanding and the nature of the feedback given to students. We also scaled the pursuits of students during instruction including the nature of the conversation that occurred among students, the nature of their collaboration, and their overall engagement in lesson activities. The scaled data from each aspect of instruction were distilled into a composite index for instruction with the single underlying dimension of teaching mathematics for understanding. In this study, we found that half of the MiC teacher/student groups in Districts 1 and 2 experienced teaching for understanding while the other half experienced more conventional pedagogy. Furthermore, 5th-grade teachers were more likely to support reform instruction, with 8th-grade teachers moving in that direction more than the 6th- or 7th-grade teachers.

The quality of instruction had a positive effect on student performance. Although there was considerable variation in CA scores, MiC teacher/student groups who experienced teaching for understanding tended to score higher than other groups. For example, four of the six MiC teacher/student groups in Grade 6 in 1998–1999 with mean CA scores above 265 experienced instruction that was reflective of teaching mathematics for understanding (see Table 10.4).

The instruction composite variable accounted for the three intervening variables in the structural research model. Each of these variables and their relationship to CA are described below.

Table 10.4 Classroom achievement for Grade 6 MiC teacher/student groups in Districts 1 and 2 in 1998–1999, by the quality of instruction experienced

District/teacher ID	Sample	Mean	SD	Confidence interval	
				Lower	Upper
Reflective of Teaching for Understanding					
District 1					
33	43	267.5	58.1	250.2	284.9
67	24	266.1	45.4	248.0	284.3
78	22	312.0	17.5	304.7	319.3
District 2					
69	41	281.6	40.1	269.3	293.9
Limited Attention to Conceptual Understanding					
District 1					
—					
District 2					
52	41	204.0	41.7	191.2	216.8
85	49	283.0	34.8	273.2	292.7
Lessons Focused on Procedures or Underdeveloped Lessons					
District 1					
38	44	292.0	56.2	275.4	308.6
73	29	209.8	38.1	195.9	223.6
District 2					
83	40	201.2	34.3	190.6	211.8

Pedagogical decisions

The pedagogical decisions teachers make prior to and during instruction have a direct impact on student learning. These decisions include deliberate advanced planning such as emphases given during instruction and other modifications of the intended curriculum. Pedagogical decisions also include teachers' on-the-spot interactive decisions made during instruction. Therefore, the variable *Pedagogical Decisions* in the structural research model represents teachers' decisions in defining the actual curriculum.

Of the eight aspects of instruction related to pedagogical decisions, three were well correlated with the instruction composite variable: two involving lesson planning (instructional formats that promoted classroom discourse for the purpose of the lesson and student activities that promoted discussion, problem solving, and reflection on lesson content) and one involving classroom interaction (teachers' interactive decisions). The effect of these three aspects of instruction on student performance is illustrated with data from Grade 6 MiC teacher/student groups in 1998–1999 (see Table 10.5). The ratings scaled for each teacher's pedagogical decisions reflect a strong relationship to the quality of instruction. This implies that when teachers' pedagogical decisions align with teaching mathematics for understanding, the decisions have a positive impact on student achievement.

Classroom events

Pedagogical methods that encourage students to become actively involved in their learning as well as other teacher behaviors during teaching undoubtedly influence student outcomes. Encouraging students to look for relationships among mathematical ideas, extend and apply mathematics in novel situations, reflect on their thinking and articulate it to others, and make mathematics their own are significant elements in teaching and learning mathematics with understanding. These critical elements of classroom interaction should be interwoven as commonplace events during class time. The variable *Classroom Events* in the structural research model includes the ways lessons were presented and developed, the nature of the inquiry during instruction, and the nature of teachers' classroom assessment practices.

The effect of *Classroom Events* on student performance is illustrated with data from Grade 6 MiC teacher/student groups in 1998–1999 (see Table 10.6).

The ratings scaled for classroom events reflect a strong relationship with the quality of instruction. This implies that when classroom events align with teaching mathematics for understanding, they have an important impact on student achievement.

Table 10.5 Relationship between pedagogical decisions and classroom achievement for Grade 6 MiC teacher/student groups in Districts 1 and 2 in 1998–1999

District/teacher ID	Pedagogical decisions			
	Forms of instruction that promote classroom discourse for the purpose of the lesson[1]	Student activities that promote discussion, problem solving, and reflection on lesson content[2]	Interactive teacher decisions during instruction[3]	Mean CA score
Reflective of Teaching for Understanding				
District 1				
33	2.50	2.50	4	267.5
67	3.75	3.75	3	266.1
78	3.75	3.75	4	312.0
District 2				
69	5.00	2.50	5	281.6
Limited Attention to Conceptual Understanding				
District 1				
–				
District 2				
52	2.50	2.50	3	204.0
85	2.50	3.75	3	283.0
Lessons Focused on Procedures or Underdeveloped Lessons				
District 1				
38	2.50	2.50	1	292.0
73	2.50	2.50	2	209.8
District 2				
83	2.50	2.50	3	201.2

[1] Scaled from 1-student discourse seldom planned to 4-substantive conversation planned; weighted to a 5-point scale
[2] Scaled from 1-discussion, problem solving, reflection seldom planned to 4-dominant presence in lesson plan; weighted to a 5-point scale
[3] Scaled from 1-decisions least aligned with teaching for understanding to 5-most aligned with teaching for understanding

Student pursuits

In reform recommendations, student involvement is characterized by verbs such as "explore, justify, represent, solve, construct, discuss, use, investigate, describe, develop, and predict" (NCTM, 1989, p. 17). Expectations for students to express their thinking, discuss interpretations of problem situations, consider different levels and qualities of solution strategies shared in the group, and answer questions from others about their reasoning are evident and valued. The variable *Student Pursuits* in the structural

Table 10.6 Relationship between classroom events and classroom achievement for Grade 6 MiC teacher/student groups in Districts 1 and 2 in 1998–1999

District/teacher ID	Classroom events								Mean CA score
	Mathematical interaction					Classroom assessment practice			
	Lesson presentation and development	Nature of inquiry	Nature of student explanations	Elicitation of multiple strategies	Lesson closure, reflection, or summary	Type of evidence sought	Feedback coherence and purpose	Content of feedback	
District 1				Reflective of Teaching for Understanding					
33	5[a]	4[b]	3.97[c]	2.81[d]	1.67[e]	4[f]	3[g]	4[h]	267.5
67	4	3	3.70	3.75	3.33	3	3	4	266.1
78	3	4	3.67	1.75	1.67	2	2	3	312.0
District 2									
69	5	5	3.88	3.75	3.33	3	3	4	281.6
				Limited Attention to Conceptual Understanding					
District 1									
—									
District 2									
52	4	3	2.50	2.09	1.67	2	2	3	204.0
85	3	3	2.85	2.33	1.67	2	2	2	283.0

Lessons Focused on Procedures or Underdeveloped Lessons

	a	b	c	d	e	f	g	h	
District 1									
38	2	1	2.40	1.66	1.67	1	2	3	292.0
73	2	2	2.22	1.53	1.67	1	2	2	209.8
District 2									
83	3	3	1.67	1.25	1.67	2	2	2	201.2

[a] Mean rating scaled from 1-no formal presentation to 6-emphasis on conceptual understanding with active participation by students; weighted to a 5-point scale

[b] Mean rating scaled from 1-limited to lower order thinking to 4-in-depth exploration of mathematics; weighted to a 5-point scale

[c] Mean rating scaled from 1-answers only to 3-focus on mathematical processes; weighted to a 5-point scale

[d] Mean rating scaled from 1-strategies not elicited to 4-strategies substantive element of instruction; weighted on a 5-point scale

[e] Mean rating scaled from 1-limited opportunities to 3-frequent opportunities; weighted to a 5-point scale

[f] Mean rating scaled from 1-limited evidence to 5-principled process orientation

[g] Mean rating from 1-no feedback to 5-toward student self-assessment

[h] Mean rating from 1-feedback withheld or misleading to 5-concept-directed feedback

research model included the nature of student–student conversation, the nature of students' collaborative working relationships, and the overall level of student engagement in the lesson.

The effect of *Student Pursuits* on student performance is illustrated with data from Grade 6 MiC teacher/student groups in 1998–1999 (see Table 10.7). The ratings scaled for student pursuits reflect a strong relationship to the quality of instruction. This implies that when students are discussing their work, collaboratively working in lesson activities, and actively participating in lessons, their actions have a positive impact on student achievement.

As these data illustrate, students in MiC teacher/student groups had

Table 10.7 Relationship between student pursuits and classroom achievement for Grade 6 MiC teacher/student groups in Districts 1 and 2 in 1998–1999

District/teacher ID	Student pursuits			
	Nature of student–student conversation[1]	Nature of students' collaborative working relationships[2]	Overall level of engagement[3]	Mean CA score
Reflective of Teaching for Understanding				
District 1				
33	2.23	2.36	4.03	267.5
67	3.05	2.64	4.59	266.1
78	3.25	3.75	4.75	312.0
District 2				
69	3.34	2.91	4.59	281.6
Limited Attention to Conceptual Understanding				
District 1				
–				
District 2				
52	2.09	2.19	3.96	204.0
85	2.50	2.78	4.29	283.0
Lessons Focused on Procedures or Underdeveloped Lessons				
District 1				
38	1.53	1.41	3.61	292.0
73	1.25	1.25	1.95	209.8
District 2				
83	2.33	1.61	4.11	201.2

[1] Mean rating scaled from 1-conversation not encouraged to 4-substantive conversation; weighted to a 5-point scale
[2] Mean rating scaled from 1-no collaboration to 4-substantive collaboration; weighted to a 5-point scale
[3] Mean rating scaled from 1-disruptive engagement to 4-widespread engagement; weighted to a 5-point scale

different instructional experiences as they learned mathematics. When instruction reflected teaching mathematics for understanding, student achievement tended to be higher than performance for groups who experienced conventional pedagogy.

Opportunity to learn with understanding

As described in Chapter 6, the composite variable opportunity to learn with understanding (OTL*u*) was characterized by the curricular content taught, the decisions in defining the actual curriculum, and four aspects of instruction that promote understanding: the development of conceptual understanding through the teacher's active support of classroom inter-actions that promote students' conjectures and students' exploration of connections in mathematics and between mathematics and their life experiences (Shafer, 2005b). All six aspects of OTL*u* were well correlated with the OTL*u* composite variable. By linking teachers' decisions in defin-ing the actual curricular content with classroom interactions that promote teaching mathematics for understanding, we were able to differentiate variation in the OTL*u* students experienced.

Nearly three-fourths of the MiC teacher/student groups in the first two study years and half of the MiC groups in the third year created classroom cultures characteristic of OTL*u*. Fifth-grade teachers more fre-quently created such cultures, with 8th-grade teachers moving in that direction more than 6th- and 7th-grade teachers. Teachers with greater experience using MiC tended to better provide more consistent OTL*u*, and their students tended to show more achievement gains (Shafer et al., 2005). Our findings suggest that the use of MiC materials enlarged and strength-ened students' OTL*u*. However, the observation data clearly show that many MiC classrooms tended to have cultures that were inconsistent with OTL*u*.

The level of OTL*u* had a positive effect on student performance. Although there was considerable variation in CA scores, MiC teacher/student groups who experienced moderate to high levels of OTL*u* tended to score higher than other groups. For example, four of the six MiC teacher/student groups in Grade 6 in 1998–1999 with mean CA scores above 265 experienced moderate to high levels of OTL*u* (see Table 10.8).

The OTL*u* composite variable accounted for one independent variable in the structural research model, *Curricular Content and Materials* and four aspects of instruction from the intervening variable *Classroom Events* that promoted understanding: the development of conceptual understand-ing, the nature of student conjectures, connections among mathematical ideas, and connections between mathematics and students' life experi-ences. Each of these variables and their relationship to CA are described below.

Table 10.8 Classroom achievement for Grade 6 MiC teacher/student groups in
Districts 1 and 2 in 1998–1999, by the opportunity to learn with
understanding experienced

				Confidence interval	
District/teacher ID	*Sample*	*Mean*	*SD*	*Lower*	*Upper*
Moderate to High Levels of OTLu					
District 1					
33	43	267.5	58.1	250.2	284.9
67	24	266.1	45.4	248.0	284.3
78	22	312.0	17.5	304.7	319.3
District 2					
69	41	281.6	40.1	269.3	293.9
Low to Limited Levels of OTLu					
District 1					
38	44	292.0	56.2	275.4	308.6
73	29	209.8	38.1	195.9	223.6
District 2					
52	41	204.0	41.7	191.2	216.8
83	40	201.2	34.3	190.6	211.8
85	49	283.0	34.8	273.2	292.7

Curricular content and materials

We gathered information on the mathematics content students had an
opportunity to learn and the nature of modifications teachers made to the
curriculum they used. The effect of these aspects of OTLu on student
performance is illustrated with data from Grade 6 MiC teacher/student
groups in 1998–1999 (see Table 10.9). The ratings scaled for the content
each teacher taught and the modifications the teacher made to the curriculum generally reflect a positive relationship to moderate to high levels of
OTLu. This implies that when teachers used MiC as recommended in
teacher support materials with few modifications, their decisions had a
positive impact on student achievement.

Although we gathered information on the content of the actual curriculum, we also explored the way the curricular materials were taught for
understanding. In doing so, we went beyond measures of content coverage to link four aspects of *Classroom Events* that promote understanding
to the content. The effect of these aspects of OTLu on student performance is illustrated with data from Grade 6 MiC teacher/student groups in
1998–1999 (see Table 10.10). The ratings scaled for these aspects of *Classroom Events* generally reflect a positive relationship to moderate to high
levels of OTLu. This implies that when teachers emphasized conceptual

Table 10.9 Relationship between curricular content and materials and class-room achievement for Grade 6 MiC teacher/student groups in Districts 1 and 2 in 1998–1999

| District/teacher ID | Curricular content and materials | | Mean CA score |
	Curricular content[1]	Modifications to curricular materials[2]	
Moderate to High Levels of OTLu			
District 1			
33	6.0	6	267.5
67	6.0	5	266.1
78	3.6	2	312.0
District 2			
69	4.8	5	281.6
Low to Limited Levels of OTLu			
District 1			
38	1.2	2	292.0
73	3.6	3	209.8
District 2			
52	4.8	4	204.0
83	2.4	2	201.2
85	6.0	5	283.0

[1] Scaled from 1-vast content heavily laden with vocabulary and prescribed algorithms to 5-comprehensive, integrated curriculum with attention to all content areas; weighted to a 6-point scale
[2] Scaled from 1-curriculum presented in a haphazard way that did not adhere to a text and did not emphasize connections among topics to 6-curriculum modified in ways that enhanced conceptual development of the content

understanding, allowed students to conjecture about the mathematics they were learning, and emphasized connections, their actions had a positive impact on student achievement.

As these data illustrate, students in MiC teacher/student groups had different opportunities to learn mathematics with understanding. When teachers used MiC as recommended with few modifications and classroom events reflected teaching mathematics for understanding, student achievement tended to be higher than performance for groups whose teachers used MiC in limited ways, modified MiC extensively with supplemental materials, and taught in ways less aligned with teaching for understanding.

School capacity

As described in Chapter 5, school capacity is the collective power of the school staff to improve student achievement. Through examining school capacity, we identified and described social and institutional factors that

Table 10.10 Relationship between classroom events that promote teaching for understanding and classroom achievement for Grade 6 MiC teacher/student groups in Districts 1 and 2 in 1998–1999

| District/teacher ID | Classroom events that promote teaching for understanding | | | | | Mean CA score |
	Development of conceptual understanding[1]	Nature of student conjectures[2]	Connections among mathematical ideas[3]	Connections between mathematics and students' lives[4]	

Moderate to High Levels of OTLu

District 1					
33	5.07	3.17	3.38	3.34	267.5
67	3.66	3.00	2.84	3.78	266.1
78	4.20	3.00	5.40	4.00	312.0
District 2					
69	5.00	4.25	3.26	5.24	281.6

Low to Limited Levels of OTLu

District 1					
38	2.00	2.00	1.67	2.88	292.0
73	2.16	2.00	2.34	2.88	209.8
District 2					
52	3.26	2.25	2.75	4.00	204.0
83	3.44	2.36	2.57	3.72	201.2
85	3.86	2.57	2.57	4.28	283.0

[1] Mean rating scaled from 1-lesson did not promote conceptual understanding to 4-continual focus on building connections or linking procedural knowledge with conceptual knowledge; weighted to a 6-point scale

[2] Mean rating scaled from 1-no conjectures observed to 4-students made generalizations about mathematical ideas; weighted to a 6-point scale

[3] Mean rating scaled from 1-mathematical topic was presented in isolation of other topics to 4-mathematical topic of the lesson was explored in enough detail for students to think about relationships among mathematical topics; weighted to a 6-point scale

[4] Mean rating scaled from 1-connections not apparent to 3-connections clearly apparent; weighted to a 6-point scale

influenced student learning. We looked at variables that ranged from the vision for teaching and learning mathematics and administrative support to teacher influence over school policy and collaboration among teachers. We created a composite index to scale teachers' perceptions of school capacity, which included levels from Level 1—Very low school capacity to Level 5—High level of school capacity.

As we looked at the perceptions of school capacity for all study teachers, we found that District 1 teachers were less likely to perceive high levels of school capacity than teachers in the other districts (Shafer, 2005c). Sixth-grade teachers were far less likely to perceive high school capacity than 5th- and 7th-grade teachers in the first year. In the second year, one-half of the study teachers (all middle school) perceived high school capacity, and in the third year, 8th-grade teachers were more likely than 7th-grade teachers to perceive high school capacity.

Support environment

The school capacity composite variable accounted for the one independent variable, *Support Environment*, in the structural research model. Schools vary in their efforts to promote quality instructional experiences for all students and to develop and support professional communities for staff. Successful schools develop cultures that include both high expectations for student learning (as well as normative practices of staff that increase the likelihood of meeting those expectations) and structural features such as sustained time for collaborative discussions, observation, instructional planning, and staff development. In the variable *Support Environment* both school cultural and structural conditions were considered.

Overall, one-fourth of the MiC teachers perceived a high quality of support environment and one-fourth perceived an average support environment. However, MiC teachers in Districts 1 and 2 varied greatly, with 70% indicating an average level of support in District 1 in contrast to 61% indicating a high level of support in District 2.

To illustrate the impact of the support environment on student achievement, we describe the school capacity perceived by two 6th-grade teachers in 1998–1999 whose students had comparable achievement at the end of Grade 5 (Shafer et al., 2005). Ms Gollen in District 1 perceived moderately high school capacity, reporting that she received strong administrative support in terms of clearly communicated expectations, support for selecting instructional materials, changes in instructional practice, and changes in policy. However, she felt that she had an average level of influence in planning and teaching mathematics and curriculum. Although formal meetings were held for mathematics teachers, teachers met informally on a limited basis to discuss mathematics curriculum and instruction. Substitute time was allotted for external professional development. Ms Gollen was the only 6th-grade MiC teacher in her school, and she did not have the opportunity to collaborate with other teachers in the school or in the district who were implementing MiC.

Ms Redling in District 2 perceived high school capacity, stating that she received very strong administrative support in terms of clearly communicated expectations, support for selecting instructional materials, changes in instructional practice, and changes in policy. She felt that she had a high level of influence over educational policies related to curriculum and to planning and teaching mathematics. Ms Redling reported that numerous professional development opportunities were available in the school, and the principal allotted substitute time for external professional development. During formal meetings, mathematics teachers on her teaching team discussed content, instructional and assessment methods, and program evaluation. Teachers also met informally to discuss a variety of topics.

Two things are of interest in this discussion of the support environment. First, students of these teachers made transitions from elementary to middle schools in which the structural and cultural conditions were different from what they experienced in elementary grades. However, despite changes in these conditions, the performance of Ms Redling's students increased significantly, in comparison to the modest decline in the performance of Ms Gollen's students. The transition from elementary to middle schools may have influenced students in some schools and not others. Second, Ms Gollen was the only 6th-grade MiC teacher in her school, and she reported infrequent meetings with other mathematics teachers. This contrasts with Ms Redling's participation in meetings with mathematics teachers on her teaching team on a regular basis. Although this was also the first year Ms Redling taught MiC 6th-grade units, other teachers on the team had taught these units. Their discussions not only included content but instructional and assessment methods. This type of collaboration and support likely supported the quality of instruction and OTLu her students experienced and mitigated the impact of students' transition from elementary to middle schools.

In this study, we found that when teachers implemented MiC in isolation in their schools, particularly at Grade 6, CA increased slightly or modestly declined. However, CA increased, sometimes significantly, when teachers regularly collaborated in meaningful discussions about mathematics curriculum, instruction, and assessment.

As this discussion of the variable *Support Environment* illustrates, differences in teachers' perceptions of school capacity helped us to identify other factors that affected student achievement.

Other independent variables

Two other independent variables were included in the structural research model, *Teacher Knowledge* and *Teacher Professional Responsibility*. However, because of the difficulty in gathering data to examine these variables, we were unable to draw conclusions about the relationship of these variables to student achievement. In the next paragraphs, we describe the ways we defined these variables and what we came to understand about study teachers with respect to these variables.

Teacher Knowledge

The variable *Teacher Knowledge* in the structural model accounted for (a) the teachers' developing understanding of pedagogical methods for teaching broader, deeper, and sometimes new mathematical content, and (b) the opportunities teachers had to learn mathematics content in ways that are more compatible with the processes reform-based curricula require of students.

No direct measure of the variable *Teacher Knowledge* was included in the data collection for this study because districts were unwilling for us to test teacher knowledge in direct ways. However, through teacher interviews and journal entries we learned ways teachers were developing knowledge for teaching comprehensive mathematical content in depth (Shafer, 2004a). For example, when planning to teach an individual MiC lesson, Ms Heath worked through all lesson problems, then read the teacher guide to check whether she understood the intended meaning of the problems and the purpose and direction of the lesson (Seventh grade; Heath, Interview 5/11/99). Over time, teachers felt that they better understood the goals of MiC, stating, for example, that they were more able to see the "whole picture" in a unit, select portions of lessons that they wanted to emphasize, and focus more on the mathematics than the contexts.

Teachers also learned how to introduce and work with new mathematical tools that supported students' thinking such as the ratio table. The tentative nature of this knowledge, however, is illustrated in this teacher's request:

> Please tell me how to explain p. 52 Section B The Ratio Table in *Number Tools*. The students and I understand doubling and adding. However, we want to know which columns to add if they are not in bold type.
>
> (Fifth grade, Murphy, Journal entry 1/6/98)

In addition, MiC teachers were learning how to teach mathematics content in ways that emphasized conceptual understanding and supported student reasoning. For example, some teachers resisted the temptation to teach traditional algorithms for fraction operations, while others found it essential before teaching the two MiC units specifically designed to build on students' informal knowledge of fractions and to develop conceptual understanding of operations with fractions. Other teachers reported that it was difficult to teach for connections among the rational number concepts of ratio, fractions, decimals, and percent, for example, because they had to "rethink how to present this to students" (Sixth grade, Gollen, Journal entry 2/11/99). Furthermore, teachers wrote about their lack of pedagogical content knowledge for new content, such as their ability to "anticipate the students' success or difficulties" and to understand "students' reluctance to answer questions" (Sixth grade, Gollen, Journal entry 2/22/99; fifth grade, Murphy, Journal entry 1/22/98).

Over time, teachers reported that they were becoming more facilitative during instruction and that instructional pacing was much improved. Teachers noted differences in student engagement during instruction after studying MiC for one year. Teachers had developed ways to allow students to do more mathematical thinking in class, as described by Ms Keeton:

> Before we open the book, I read the questions and ask them if there are any questions on each lesson question. Do you understand what it's asking for? What does that mean? How are you going to do that? And we'll go through all of the pages that I want them to do for that day. Then they actually start their assignment. I found that to be much more successful.
>
> (Eighth grade, MiC, Keeton, Interview 10/23/98)

Teachers struggled with giving students time to think about instructional tasks, reason out strategies, and determine solutions. Teachers gradually developed ways for students to do the mathematical work *and* discuss various strategies, as one teacher noted: "I learned to introduce the lesson, ask students to work on a few problems, reconvene to discuss the content with the whole class, and repeat that during the lesson" (Sixth-grade, Dillard, Personal communication 2/26/98). Teachers also worked at improving the quality of group work and students' written work.

Thus, throughout our extensive set of data, we found evidence that teachers' knowledge was changing: their understanding of the mathematics, presentation of the mathematics, pedagogical content knowledge, and instructional strategies, all of which are central to effective instruction, were being developed and extended as teachers taught MiC.

Beyond what we learned about teacher knowledge through qualitative data, we attempted to examine teacher knowledge through questions about teachers' conceptions of the nature of mathematics and the teaching and learning of mathematics. While not a direct measure of teacher knowledge, the questionnaire data provided information about how teachers characterized mathematics and effective methods of instruction in mathematics. Our attempt to examine teacher knowledge is consistent with the methodologies reported in other studies (e.g., Schmidt, et al., 2001). Two-thirds of the study teachers believed that the nature of mathematics was both static (a collection of concepts and skills used to obtain answers to problems) and dynamic (thinking in a logical, inquisitive manner used to develop understanding; Romberg et al., 2004). Most teachers agreed with situating mathematics in everyday situations, that basic skills should be learned before students can generalize, and that students would not learn mathematics well if they used calculators and worked in small groups. Generally, teachers agreed that their primary goal was to help students master basic concepts and procedures, instruction should be based on their knowledge of student understanding, more emphasis should be given to mental computation and estimation, and discussion, problem solving, and connections were important elements of instruction. Teachers were neutral about whether it was more important to cover fewer topics in depth and whether instruction should include step-by-step directions or open-ended tasks. In addition, teachers were ambivalent about whether more algebra, geometry, probability and statistics should be introduced in the curriculum and whether teaching a concept should begin with an example or model. Furthermore, while some teachers believed that mastery of facts should precede further study of mathematics and that students should write about how they solved problems, others disagreed. Thus, the responses of study teachers reflected an inconsistent notion of the nature of mathematics and ambiguity about how students best learn mathematics, yet their responses included some positive beliefs about reform pedagogy.

In summary, although no direct measures of the variable *Teacher Knowledge* were conducted, we found that teachers were learning to teach different mathematics content in ways that allowed students to do more of the mathematical work, discuss ideas, and work collaboratively. However, questionnaire data indicated that teachers had inconsistent notions of the nature of mathematics and best ways for students to learn mathematics, even though they agreed with some more reform-oriented ideas about pedagogy.

Teacher Professional Responsibility

The variable *Teacher Professional Responsibility* included the ways in which teachers learned about new curricula and approaches in mathematics teaching and learning, specifically, teachers' opportunities to read professional literature, to participate in in-service sessions, and to attend professional meetings. We attempted to gather information about teacher professional responsibility through questionnaires and interviews. However, teachers' questionnaire responses led us to believe that teachers did not interpret terms in ways we had anticipated. For example, when asked about the subject and frequency of formal meetings with other teachers in the school, some responses reflected district-level meetings, and when asked about professional collaboration in the school, responses to questionnaire items and interview questions gave conflicting information. Therefore, we did not pursue further analysis relative to this variable.

However, as we explained in earlier chapters, we did learn that the need for professional development was critical, which is underscored by the following examples. In District 2 in the second and third years of data collection, MiC teachers were given one day of release time per month in order to collaborate on planning to teach MiC units. These collaborative times were effective for changing instruction, for instance: "Having the MiC days to prepare, discuss, and work through the units is very beneficial" (Eighth grade, MiC, Teague, Journal entry 4/29/99). Teachers in District 1 did not have such opportunities. Two teachers in particular requested support beyond what the study provided in the summer professional development institutes. Because Ms Gollen was the only MiC 6th-grade mathematics teacher in her school, she did not have the opportunity to collaborate with other teachers who were implementing MiC. Our study on-site observer commented that Ms Gollen had difficulty discerning the alignment of lessons with the unit goals, presenting lesson content, and orchestrating classroom discussions. She recommended mentoring on a regular basis and stated that many teachers would benefit from this kind of interaction (Diver, Observer comments 3/18/99). Ms Reichers, the only 8th-grade MiC teacher in her school, requested that a consultant teach her class while she observed the lesson, a request that was accommodated by the district mathematics specialist. Ms Reichers found this to be a worthwhile experience that influenced her teaching. These examples suggest that teachers benefit from interaction with other MiC teachers, especially when they can have in depth discussions on planning and teaching MiC.

In summary, although we were aware that teachers' professional responsibility varied and professional development opportunities for teachers were important considerations, we were unable to capture consistent data from questionnaires and interviews to scale what we had learned about the variable *Teacher Professional Responsibility* in a meaningful way.

Summary

In this set of studies, considerable information was gathered on a large set of variables in addition to the use of curricular materials. Our intent was to gather data on 14 variables in 5 categories based on our original research model. However, for practical reasons we created a simplified model that included only 5 composite variables derived from data collected on many of the original variables. For example, the composite scale for instruction (I) combined data collected on the original variables *Pedagogical Decisions, Classroom Events*, and *Student Pursuits*. Similarly, the composite scale for classroom achievement (CA) combined data from the four grade-level assessments on *Knowledge and Understanding* and the four grade-level assessments on *Application*.

For some of the variables in the original model we were unable to collect data that could be scaled. For example, it was politically unfeasible to collect data on *Teacher Knowledge* and practically difficult to collect data on *Further Pursuits*. Also, while we were able to collect reasonable data on some variables in the original model we elected not to use the information in the simplified model. For example, *Student Background* data on attitudes, mathematical reasoning, and ethnicity was gathered and the variability noted. Similarly, for *Social Context* the variability of the four districts in the study was noted.

Nevertheless, the variables in the structural research model for the study gave us a framework for the development of instruments and the creation of indices used to answer the three research questions posed for the study.

Answer to Question 3

Overall, the achievement of students in the year prior to being studied was the best predictor of student performance in a given year. When prior achievement was accounted for, the degree of implementation of MiC was a significant predictor of student achievement. Clearly, variations in the quality of instruction, the opportunity to learn with understanding, and the capacity of schools to support mathematics teaching and learning affected the cultures in which student learning was situated, and, therefore, student achievement.

Chapter 11

What we learned from the research and the implications for curriculum evaluations

The purpose of our summative evaluation was to document the impact on student achievement of using the standards-based middle-school mathematics curriculum *Mathematics in Context*, to compare that achievement with the performance of students who studied conventional curricula, and to examine factors that contributed to student opportunity to learn with understanding. The challenges we faced in conducting this comparative longitudinal research in the reality of school life seemed daunting at times. As numerous as these challenges were, however, we were able to follow many students longitudinally, collect rich observation and achievement data, and record teacher accounts of what transpired in study classes. In this chapter we comment on some of the things we learned from conducting the evaluation, and then reflect on the implications of our experiences for future summative evaluations of standards-based curricula.

What we learned

To summarize what we have learned, we have chosen to focus on five aspects of the study: (1) the study design, instrument construction, and methods of data analysis; (2) time and resources; (3) working in large urban districts with administrators and support staff; (4) the students in the study; and (5) the teachers who allowed us to gather information from them and in their classrooms (Romberg & Shafer, 2005).

What we learned about the study design

We found that basing the study on a structural model and quantifying the variables in the model was a reasonable way to conduct studies of the implementation of curricula in schools. In particular, the logic of the sequence of variables from "Prior" to "Consequent" was reasonable. Furthermore, the identification of potential variables gave us a starting point for the development of measures for the study. However, we found that many of the "Independent" and "Intervening" variables were composites of related sub-variables. For example, the variable *Classroom Events* represented the interactions among the teacher and students that promoted learning mathematics with understanding. These events arose from a learning environment in which students explored mathematics and were encouraged to make sense of mathematics. Data were therefore gathered on six sub-variables: lesson presentation and development; nature of mathematical inquiry during instruction; teachers' interactive decisions; nature of students' explanations; elicitation of multiple strategies; and lesson closure, reflection, or summary. For analysis purposes, measures of the variables and sub-variables were usually statistically collinear. Nevertheless, intellectually, the sub-variables were different and, although information about them was aggregated into a single index, thereby losing some of the distinct character of events in particular classrooms, the measures of the sub-variables could also be disaggregated in order to describe particular events or aspects of instructional approaches.

Quantifying the variables in a structural model was hard work. We were able to create good measures for many of the variables. In the year prior to the study, we identified and developed all the instruments we planned to use and spent considerable resources in piloting their use, in developing scoring routines, and in scaling the resultant data. However, we were unable to develop adequate measures for the mathematical background of both students and teachers in the model. For students, we decided to use the data from district standardized tests as a measure of student prior mathematical knowledge. However, the schools used different tests and no item data were available. In fact, the best we could do was use each student's percentile rank as a score, assuming that the norm-populations of the various tests were similar. Also, assessing a teacher's mathematical background and knowledge proved to be politically difficult. While we could test students, we could not test teachers. The questionnaires we used failed to capture the essential features of their mathematical knowledge.

For analysis purposes, because collinearity across indices for many of the variables posed a serious interpretation problem, a simplified model was designed with five composite variables. The simplified model proved to be important in this study. It described the relationship between variation in classroom achievement (CA), aggregated by strand or total performance and variations in preceding achievement (PA), method of instruction (I), opportunity to learn with understanding (OTL*u*), and school capacity (SC). These composite indices, based on one or more subscales developed for each variable in the original model, were then created and used in further subdividing and describing treatment groups and in regression analysis to determine the impact of the variables on student achievement.

The creation of composite CA scale via a subcontract with the Australian Council for Educational Research as the primary outcome measure for the longitudinal study was critical. Six levels of achievement were derived from the typical set of knowledge, skills, and understandings students demonstrated when they engaged with the test items (Turner & O'Connor, 2005). Also, the CA progress maps provided pictorial representations of the variable of "mathematical competence". Progress maps were useful in monitoring changes in student achievement over time and in comparison of achievement for various groups such as all students at a particular grade level in a particular year, or by district, curriculum taught, teacher/ student group, gender, and ethnic group.

Data to test the relationships between variables in the research model were collected over three years, and analysis included eight grade-level-by-year studies, three cross-grade comparisons, three cross-year comparisons, and longitudinal studies for groups of students over the three years of the study. We found that we were overly ambitious. We simply did not have the resources to adequately gather data on all the variables in several school districts over three years.

In fact, our analysis plans had to be modified. Initially, we had planned to carry out structural equations to examine the relationship of the variables in the structural model with the classroom as the unit of analysis for the eight grade-level-by-year studies in classes using MiC across all four districts. Instead, because we only had complete data on all the variables in two districts, we chose to make descriptive comparisons using student performance on the CA scale and its content subscales as the dependent variables. These comparisons made it very obvious that there was considerable variation in student performance in every comparison made.

To examine differences in CA in classrooms in which MiC was implemented and in classrooms in which conventional curricula were used in the same school districts, a quasi-experimental study was carried out. We learned that quasi-experimental studies, while an attractive alternative to true experiments, are unsatisfactory because there is no way to control all the sources of variation in classrooms. As illustrated in this study, no matter how one examined the experimental units, they were not equivalent. Many MiC teachers nominally implemented MiC in their classrooms, and in a few conventional classrooms, instruction was hardly conventional. This led to restricting comparisons to three treatment groups based on teacher levels on the Instruction and OTLu composite variables. In conclusion, we believe using a structural model and quantifying the variables in the model is the best way to conduct studies of the implementation of curricula in schools.

What we learned about time and resources

As we commented in Chapter 2, to carry out the proposed study required considerably more resources than NSF was able to allocate for the project. We simply did not have the resources, staff, and time to do everything that could, or probably should, have been done. The initial grant (NSF Grant No. REC 0553889) provided funds for developing instruments, gathering information, and establishing the database. Having an initial year to develop and test instruments was invaluable. However, when we started to collect data, we did not have the funds to hire observers for two of the four districts, and while we paid participating teachers a minimal stipend for completing logs we should have paid them more.

Creating indices to capture variation among study participants was an arduous task. For example, for each index used in the composite index Instruction, several levels were identified and described through extensive discussions and literature reviews on differences between conventional approaches and teaching mathematics for understanding. Levels were further refined and additional levels were integrated as data from 5th-grade study teachers in District 1 were reviewed. Each index was subsequently revised to be inclusive of all data from 6th- through 8th-grade teachers in District 1 and data from all teachers in District 2 were reviewed. Additional codes were sometimes necessary when working with data from multiple study years. When they were added, the entire data set had to be reread in light of the new codes.

Our data collection was thorough and diverse. We worked toward having multiple sources of data to triangulate our findings. For example, for 14 of the indices used for the composite index Instruction, we summarized information from ratings on the observation instrument, written evidence from observers, checklists in teaching logs, and teachers' journal entries. Collating, coding, summarizing, and displaying the data in meaningful ways was difficult. In addition, a written summary was created for every teacher for each index to later be used in describing what we learned about the instruction students experienced for each study year. Working with multiple data sources enabled us to get a deeper understanding of the instruction that transpired in study classrooms, but summarizing it was time-intensive and required a multiple-step process for each aspect of instruction.

The analysis of the data was funded by a supplementary grant (NSF Grant No. REC 0087511). With these funds we were able to organize the data and prepare most of the preliminary technical reports summarizing various aspects of the information. However, we ran out of funds before we could prepare the eight summary monographs or this book. Modest funds for the writing of the monographs and this book were provided from Wisconsin Center for Education Research's royalty account and personal funds along with support from Northern Illinois University. The lack of funds meant that the writing of the summary documents only happened after other academic responsibilities were met.

What we learned by conducting research in large urban school districts

Three of the four school districts with whom we worked were large districts in urban settings, two of which served predominantly low-income populations. When we designed this study, we wanted to work in such school districts because of the political pressure to help these struggling schools. Also, NSF asked us to work in settings where they had invested in mathematics and science reform. Additionally, it is considered too easy to study educational phenomena in affluent suburban districts. Most programs will work in that environment, but many programs do not transfer to an impoverished urban environment. We were anxious to demonstrate that reform could happen in such schools.

Classes of students in large urban schools incur multiple changes each school year. Teachers left the study for various reasons including moving to non-study schools, being on family leave, accepting an administrative position, or resigning from participation in the study. Teachers also varied in their use of MiC. In some cases, MiC units were supplemented with other materials to the extent that MiC was subsumed by the supplementary materials. These conditions demonstrate that any contrast between MiC and conventional classrooms is more than the label associated with the text materials being used.

Parental concerns also influenced teachers' use of supplementary materials for practicing basic skills. In addition, when teachers were absent due to illness or participation in workshops, they felt that it was inappropriate to ask substitute teachers to continue MiC lessons. Instead, they prepared lessons that reinforced computational skills. These practices made the learning environments unstable for students. Teachers also compromised data collection by administering tests on days of scheduled classroom observations, neglecting to cancel planned observations when school schedules changed or when they were absent due to district professional development or to illness, and not completing teaching logs that added significantly to our understanding of what transpired in study classrooms on a daily basis.

It was our intent to study intact groups of students who stayed together over the three years of the study. However, practically this proved to be impossible in schools in these districts. For example, in District 2, 96% of the students who completed both study assessments in Grade 5 did not participate in the study for three years. In this very large urban district, mobility was a significant factor in the loss of study students. Students transferred to non-study classes in the same school or to different schools throughout the school year, which compromised our ability to follow students longitudinally.

In the large urban research districts, commitment to our study often compromised data collection. In fact, there was an unwillingness of many school districts to be involved in such a study. Many districts expressed the concern that they might be seen as withholding opportunities for learning mathematics in more powerful ways from students who continued to study conventional mathematics curricula. Also, schools using conventional curricula were difficult to find because principals did not want to be perceived as disregarding efforts to reform mathematics curriculum and instruction. Furthermore, it was difficult for large urban districts to live up to contractual commitments of keeping intact groups of students, assigning incoming 5th-grade students to classes of study teachers, selecting classes that were of average ability, and procuring standardized test scores for study students.

On the other hand, administrators in Districts 1 and 2 were very helpful in recommending retired mathematics teachers to gather classroom observation data, and our ability to contract with these observers was critical in this study. In fact, in any study of implementation, classroom observations in study schools in all research districts should be conducted, which was not possible in this study. The classroom observation instrument developed for the study allowed the observer to mark ratings on separate indices, but also to provide written evidence supporting the rating, a list of activities that transpired during the lesson and the time allotted to each, and general descriptions of the lesson. Observation reports provided pictures of the mathematical interaction that transpired in study classes based on a consistent set of variables considered during each observation. Throughout the study, classroom observation reports provided information about the content of instructional materials, the ways lessons were presented and developed, the nature of the mathematical inquiry during instruction, teachers' interactive decisions, and students' involvement in lessons.

In these large urban districts, our study was just one of many well-meaning initiatives, and implementing MiC began on a small scale, involving a few schools, before adoption by more schools in the district. District mathematics specialists were responsible for supporting teachers who were implementing MiC, along with all the other programs and initiatives in the district. Study teachers received minimal attention and support as they faced the challenges of teaching a new curriculum, and their needs for specific types of professional development, such as focusing on conceptual understanding, leading student discussion, and developing new ways to assess student learning, were not addressed. We did not have adequate resources to help study teachers, and the districts were unable to provide consistent long-term support. Study teachers were also inundated with initiatives that left them little time to devote to our research. For example, initiatives such as mandatory silent reading in every class period, supplementary materials that feature application of mathematics in the workplace, and computer-assisted drill-and-practice programs took significant amounts of class time and compromised the time necessary for students to investigate MiC unit activities. Another initiative in many districts was for 8th-grade students to complete a traditional 9th-grade algebra course. For students who did not meet the criteria for these programs, some teachers chose to use a traditional algebra text during the second semester of 8th grade rather than teaching the MiC algebra units or continue teaching units from various content strands.

Data collection was also compromised by the lack of seriousness about study assessments by teachers and students. The significance teachers and students assign to study assessments is an important consideration in conducting educational research, particularly when these assessments are used to measure growth in student performance over time. Students in this study seemed not to put forth the effort to develop reasoned responses.

The challenges we faced in conducting comparative longitudinal research in the reality of school life seemed daunting at times. Student and teacher attrition, various interpretations of commitment, treatment fidelity, and teachers' needs for professional collaboration affected data collection. These variations draw attention to the need to study the effects of the culture in which student learning is situated when analyzing the impact of standards-based curricula. Teaching mathematics happens in communities. Several social conventions such as the beliefs about the mathematics content that should be taught to all students, ability grouping as an efficient way of providing for individual differences, the validity and utility of standardized testing, and the utility of conventional grading practices were being challenged by MiC. Controlling potential sources of variation, as is done in laboratory experiments, is more difficult in classroom settings. But this does not mean that comparative research cannot be done in today's schools. Rather, as this study demonstrates, impact studies of high quality can be conducted in classroom settings when data collection and analysis are designed to take into consideration the variations encountered in these settings.

What we learned about students

Despite the difficulties in data collection, we were able to make some interesting conclusions about study students. First, we underestimated the capability of students to learn mathematics with understanding. Given the opportunity to explore some problem situations through a set of structured activities in MiC units, students did learn important mathematics with understanding. For example, 5th-grade students investigated the distortion caused by representing curved surfaces with flat maps, and 6th-grade students solved systems of linear equations. Seventh-grade students investigated periodic graphs and the tangent ratio, and 8th-grade students graphed constraints and feasible regions for inequalities. In analyses of groups of students who began a particular school year with comparable prior achievement, the results suggest that over time students who studied MiC and experienced high quality of instruction and opportunity to learn with understanding showed gains in performance.

Student learning should be seen as a product of involvement in a classroom culture. Learning with understanding is a product of interactions over time with teachers and students in a classroom environment that encourages and values exploration of problem situations, modeling, argumentation, and other mathematical processes. This type of rich mathematical interaction transpired in some study classrooms. Learning the concepts and skills in a mathematical domain requires that students be engaged in a rich set of structured activities over time. To learn the ideas in a domain, students should have the opportunity to investigate problem situations that encourage mathematization. Such situations include those that are subject to measure and quantification, that embody quantifiable change and variation, that involve specifiable uncertainty, that involve our place in space and the spatial features of the world we inhabit and construct, and that involve symbolic algorithms and more abstract structures. Also, such situations embody systematic forms of reasoning and argument to help establish the certainty, generality, consistency, and reliability of one's mathematical assertions. Some study students were able to engage in such activity. For example, in District 3, the CA performance of students was significantly higher from one year to the next, and over 50% of the students in the third year of data collection demonstrated a moderate level of mathematization, as they were able to translate either a contextualized or a non-contextualized, generally non-routine problem into mathematical terms for solution.

Learning with understanding in a domain is acquired by students gradually over time as a consequence of active engagement in structured activities designed to help students evolve from their informal ideas about a domain to more formal and abstract ways of representing and reasoning in that domain. This notion was challenging for MiC teachers. They had to resist the temptation to teach abstract procedures before building on the informal knowledge students had acquired, and they had to trust that MiC would help students become proficient in mathematical skills over time.

We found that supplementing a reform curriculum with conventional materials is not likely to result in improved student performance. What matters is that students actively engage in lessons that build on their informal ideas in particular domains and gradually move toward more abstract ways of reasoning in the domains. Students in our study have shown that they can reason about problematic situations, extend their knowledge of mathematics, and apply skills in multiple content strands.

What we learned about teachers

Convincing principals and teachers to participate in the study in the conventional treatment group proved to be difficult. Only two districts agreed to be involved in a comparative study. Principals questioned incentives for their teachers to participate as teachers using conventional curricula. They did not perceive as adequate compensation the professional development opportunities for teachers provided by the study. Teachers also expressed negative opinions about participating in groups using conventional curricula. Fewer teachers in the conventional group participated in the study over time, which compromised the comparative analyses.

Teachers felt constrained by a variety of rules and expectations that restricted their pedagogical ability. In particular, external tests, practice for such tests, and established grading practices proved to be a major impediment to changes in instruction. For example, district and state standardized tests significantly influenced the instruction of the teachers in one middle school, as large amounts of time were devoted to test preparation. In fact, this became such a serious issue that they withdrew from the study in the second semester. The principal was not convinced that mathematics education reform should be supported wholeheartedly. His interpretations of state standards led to a different approach for reaching expectations of improved student achievement.

For teachers, the MiC instructional approach represented, on the whole, a substantial departure from their prior experience and established beliefs. The content of MiC units was sometimes a challenge for teachers. In MiC, mathematical content is introduced in a different instructional sequence than in conventional middle-school curricula. For example, concepts related to percent are introduced in 5th- and 6th-grade MiC units, rather than more conventionally in 8th grade, and content traditionally reserved for high-school students such as topics in algebra and geometry is introduced in 5th- through 8th-grade units. Teachers also had to learn how to introduce and work with new mathematical tools that supported students' thinking such as the ratio table. Furthermore, few MiC teachers had experience teaching mathematics that emphasized the development of conceptual understanding and student reasoning rather than algorithms and procedures. In addition, during instruction, teachers draw on pedagogical content knowledge, but MiC teachers frequently talked about their lack of pedagogical content knowledge for new content. Teachers also expressed concern about how to help students when they could not find their own solutions to particular problems. They began to work with guiding students to complete mathematical tasks and found that they needed to develop ways to provide time for students to think about instructional tasks, reason out strategies, and determine solutions. They gradually developed ways for students to do the mathematical work and discuss various strategies, and they worked at improving the quality of group work. Teachers' own understanding of the mathematics, ways the mathematics is presented, pedagogical content knowledge for new content, and instructional strategies, all of which are central to effective instruction, were being developed as teachers taught MiC for the first time for the whole school year. Moreover, teachers struggled with grading student work. Grading was compounded when students responded in ways teachers did not anticipate. They had to refer back to the original task in the unit in order to check the worthiness of the response. Teachers using MiC developed a changed view of their students and their students' capabilities. Teachers noted that students think more about the mathematics and develop a deeper understanding of mathematics when they study MiC.

Summary

Conducting research in schools is complex and difficult. The complexity of clarifying instructional patterns in mathematics classrooms as exhibited in the daily interaction of teachers and students when a new and quite different standards-based curriculum is implemented is not easy to examine.

Implications for future summative evaluations of standards-based curricula

To summarize the implications of this study for future curriculum evaluations, we have chosen to focus on three aspects of the summative evaluations: (1) the reform vision of school mathematics; (2) study design, instrument construction, and methods of data analysis; and (3) criteria for summative evaluations.

The reform vision of school mathematics

Future summative evaluators of standards-based curricula need to remember that such curricula are based on a reform view of mathematics that differs from conventional notions of school mathematics. It would be too easy for evaluators to use tools and tests based on conventional notions to carry out such studies.

The reform view of mathematics is, above all, integrative. Every element is seen as part of a larger whole, with each part sharing reciprocal relationships with other parts. This approach stresses the acquisition of understanding by all, including the traditionally underprivileged, to the highest extent of their capability, rather than the selection and promotion of an elite group. The philosophy underlying reform mathematics simultaneously stresses erudition and common sense, integration through application, and innovation through creativity. Most importantly, it stresses the student creation of knowledge. Against this broad and ambitious view of mathematics, traditional school mathematics appears thin, artificial, and isolated.

We note as well that assessment, if intended to measure those mathematical abilities students will need in their adult lives, should move away from a focus on whether students can reproduce and use algorithms in contexts they have used continually in class drills and, instead, toward providing reliable evidence that a student can apply knowledge, *in reasonable and flexible ways*, to new, unfamiliar problem contexts. Over the course of years, students should be able to show, on those assessments, evidence of growth in the level or complexity of tasks he or she can *solve*.

The complexity of instructional issues involved in creating and sustaining classrooms that support this type of achievement include the interconnected roles of tasks; student–teacher interactions involving mathematics concepts; the reasonable, appropriate, and flexible use of technological tools in the classroom; classroom norms of collaborative and individual work; sustained professional development and teacher community; enhanced organizational support; and community and parent involvement and education. Implementing this reform vision of student achievement should mean, at a minimum, that students become mathematically literate.

The practical consequences of this vision would mean students sitting around tables or group work stations, working on collections of realistic problem-related activities, being coached by teachers, and their progress being judged through their creation of reasonable strategies, their articulation of complex concepts, and their ability to appropriately apply what they have learned in unfamiliar contexts—*equally* with the quality of their products. This shift in emphasis supports *problem solution* rather than *problem completion* and acknowledges the importance of flexible thinking and adaptable reasoning, skills needed in the rapidly changing technological world in which students live.

Study design, instrument construction, and methods of data analysis

The subcontracts we negotiated with each district contained a detailed scope of work for all study participants, and the scope of work was discussed with district personnel prior to signing the contracts. However, district administrators and on-site coordinators did not carry through with our requests for selecting schools that were representative of the district population, and teachers tended not to select classes of students with average mathematical abilities. Furthermore, some principals of schools reported to be reform-oriented were not convinced that mathematics education reform should wholeheartedly be supported, and there was no guarantee that principals whose schools were chosen as control sites did not have reform-oriented goals. Research requests were further compromised in District 2 where the on-site district coordinator for the study changed every year. This meant that each year the coordinator was unfamiliar with research goals and the complex issues that had arisen during past data collection. Moreover, the process of obtaining the agreed-to release of standardized test scores was complicated by two sets of testing in some districts with one set of data available in spring and another in fall, changes in handling of assessment data in district offices, and necessity to have student district ID numbers and, in one district, student social security numbers. These complications in research conditions were not avoided by negotiating standard subcontracts with detailed scopes of work. More substantial contractual language, and perhaps more active participation by the research team in selecting schools and classes, may be necessary in conducting research in school settings, particularly when working with districts that are distant from the research center.

We found that we were overly ambitious. We simply did not have the resources to adequately gather data from three cohort groups on all the variables in several school districts over three years. All data used to answer Question 2 were gathered in just two urban school districts. It would have been better if we had focused on one cohort of students in several districts starting at Grade 6 rather than three cohorts starting at Grades 5, 6, and 7. In fact, starting a cohort at Grade 5 in elementary schools made the cross-sectional and longitudinal studies difficult. Several factors limited our ability to follow Grade 5 students in later years. For example, in District 1, 90% of the students who completed both study assessments in Grade 5 did not participate in the study for three years, despite working with the on-site district coordinator to locate study students who did not appear on class rosters in the second and third years. Although district and school administrators agreed to schedule study students into classes of study teachers, this request was not honored. Some students who matriculated into study middle schools were not assigned to study teachers, and the on-site coordinator arranged for more teachers to participate in the study in order for the research team to follow these students longitudinally. Other study students were sprinkled among all classes for a particular study teacher. In this case, the teacher was asked to administer study assessments to those students, with the research team providing full class sets of assessments so that study students remained anonymous. Another factor played into the loss of students in District 1—an initiative in which parents chose the schools their children attended each year. Many Grade 5 students went to non-study middle schools, even though they were in traditional feeder patterns from elementary to particular middle schools.

To compare the use of a standards-based curriculum with the use of conventional materials it would be better if the materials were used in different school districts. Doing this would reduce the possibility of interference of experimental units.

We attempted in this research to measure the variables *Teacher Knowledge* and *Teacher Professional Responsibility*. Although we used extant research instruments as a basis for data collection in this study, we were unable to gather the data necessary to examine these variables in in-depth ways, and consequently we were unable to draw conclusions about the relationship of these variables to student achievement. No direct measure of the variable *Teacher Knowledge* was developed because districts were unwilling for us to test teacher knowledge in direct ways. However, as reported in Chapter 10, throughout our extensive set of data, we found evidence that teachers' knowledge was changing with respect to their understanding of the mathematics, presentation of the mathematics, pedagogical content knowledge, and instructional strategies as they taught MiC. Beyond what we learned about teacher knowledge through qualitative data, we attempted to examine teacher knowledge in ways consistent with the methodologies reported in other studies through questions about teachers' conceptions of the nature of mathematics and the teaching and learning of mathematics. Questionnaire data indicated that teachers were inconsistent in their characterizations of the nature of mathematics and best ways for students to learn mathematics, even though they agreed with some more reform-oriented ideas about pedagogy. Few researchers would argue the importance of developing a deeper understanding of teacher knowledge. However, measures of teacher knowledge are lacking, especially for use with a large number of teachers in longitudinal studies. Such measures deserve attention in the research community. In particular, a measure of teacher knowledge of mathematics is needed. As Noss and Hoyles (1996) point out, "There is a mutually constructive relationship between what teachers believe and what they do . . . a teacher's ideas about mathematics and mathematical microworlds shapes the way he or she operationalises these ideas in the classroom" (p. 201). What is needed are measures of teacher knowledge that attend to the ways teachers' beliefs permeate their actions in the classroom and ways classroom interactions affect their beliefs.

Similarly, our attempts to collect data on *Teacher Professional Responsibility* were not as in-depth as we would have liked. Although we recognized that teachers' professional responsibility varied and we found important differences in teachers' professional development opportunities, we were unable to capture consistent data from questionnaires and interviews to scale what we had learned about this variable in a meaningful way. In future studies, measures need to be developed to address this need.

The Student Attitude Inventory developed for the study included a collection of items used in previous research on student attitudes (see Romberg & Shafer, 2004a). Some items were reworded to facilitate use with middle-school students, and new items were added to reflect notions from the reform movement such as calculator use, communication, and collaboration. The instrument was pilot-tested, and analyses of reliability and validity were conducted. At the beginning of the study, attitudes were uniformly positive for all students, indicating little possibility for growth, and we were unable to identify any discernable pattern. There were no real differences between students who studied MiC and students who studied conventional curricula on the first 5 subscales (effort, confidence, interest, usefulness, and communication) and 3 (out of 16) significant differences between the groups in the general perceptions subscale. Each spring, the results suggested that the MiC group was significantly more positive than the Conventional group on only 4 of 60 items, and no significant differences were found among the three groups (MiC, MiC (Conventional), and Conventional) with respect to the first five subscales. In the general perceptions subscale, only one change in attitudes was significant, with the MiC group being significantly more positive than the MiC (Conventional) group. Although still positive, students' attitudes tended to be more negative as they progressed from 5th grade through middle school, which is consistent with previous research. Because the results were very positive for every administration of the Student Attitude Inventory, we are left wondering whether the instrument was sensitive enough to discern differences among students. Future use of the instrument in large-scale studies will help to investigate this further and perhaps make changes that will more adequately capture differences in attitudes of middle-school students over time.

Our attempt to study the variable *Further Pursuits* was mediated by low response rate from students. Unlike studies of transitions of high-school mathematics students to university mathematics courses, ways need to be developed to collect data from a large number of adolescent students (minors) as they transition into high school and must complete such instruments under parental supervision or other adult supervision with parental consent.

As expressed in Chapter 1, it is essential for summative evaluations that the instruments reflect the goals of the curriculum. In this study, the assessments needed to address the goals of MiC as well as conventional curricula. The goal of instruction using MiC is that students will acquire knowledge of concepts in the four content strands, reason at increasingly complex levels, and apply their knowledge in various situations. Therefore, it was important that the assessments assessed mathematical knowledge, reasoning, and application of mathematics. Assessments of this nature were unavailable at the time, and the development of assessments and the classroom achievement index became part of the proposal granted by NSF for this study. Because random assignment of students or classes to treatment groups was impractical, we also wanted to use norm-referenced standardized test data to look for initial differences among study classes. In our subcontracts with districts, we had already negotiated two days in the fall and four days in the spring for administering study instruments. Given this time commitment, districts asked that we did not impose additional days for standardized testing. Consequently, we asked districts to provide data from the standardized tests they administered. However, the standardized tests varied by district and only reflected students' standing with respect to different, but assumed similar, norm-populations. In future summative evaluations, it is important that research districts use a consistent form of standardized test.

In summative evaluations of the impact of standards-based curricula, it is important to develop an understanding of how the curricular materials are actually being used in the classroom and how classroom interactions promote mathematical understanding. In two of the four districts in this study, classroom observation, post-observation interviews, teaching logs, and teacher journal entries provided a basis for examining the intervening variables *Pedagogical Decisions, Classroom Events*, and *Student Pursuits*, enabling us to identify important differences among teacher/student groups in these districts. In future studies, more in-depth interviews after each observation may lead to a better understanding of the classroom learning environment. Furthermore, the resulting findings may add to the descriptions of levels for the composite indices Instruction and OTL*u* thereby continuing to build more comprehensive tools for identifying differences in intervening variables among teacher/student groups.

In today's climate of government agencies and educational researchers calling for evidence that curricular materials are "research-based," there are even more substantial needs to demonstrate that the standards-based curricula do have a positive impact on students' understanding of mathematics. District administrators often want to know the bottom line—the results on standardized measures of achievement that confirm improved student mathematical performance. However, in this study, the variations and findings we have described in this book draw attention to the need to study the effects of the culture in which student learning is situated and to look in depth at those elements that enhance classroom instruction, heighten student opportunity to learn with understanding, and build the capacity of schools to support reform curriculum and instruction. The dynamic interplay of all these variables has an impact on student learning, and as such, these variables must be considered in the evaluation of any standards-based curriculum.

As stated in Chapter 1, it is our contention that using a structural model of classroom instruction is an appropriate methodology for conducting summative evaluations of standards-based curricula. A structural model is an attempt to capture some key components and their interrelationships with respect to classroom instruction and use of curricular materials. The power of the model rests in the representation process, but also in the relationships that are shown and the predictions that can be made. In this study, the model provided a basis for gathering and interpreting information about mathematics instruction being initiated by the use of MiC. It demonstrates the belief that mathematics teaching is complex and that changes cannot be simplistically studied. As analysis proceeded, our plans for answering Question 1 had to be modified. Initially, we had planned to carry out structural equations to examine the relationship of the variables in the structural model with the classroom as the unit of analysis for the eight grade-level-by-year studies in classes using MiC across all four districts. Then from a similar structural analysis including data from classes using conventional mathematics curricula, we could answer Question 3. Instead, because we had complete data sets on all the variables in only two districts, we chose to make descriptive comparisons using student performance on the classroom achievement scale and its content subscales as the dependent variables. In future evaluation studies, we encourage the use of structural equation analysis when complete sets of data are available for all research sites.

Criteria for summative evaluations

The report of the National Research Council *On Evaluating Curricular Effectiveness* (2004) contained several suggestions evaluators should attend to when conducting summative evaluations. This is not the place to discuss all of their criteria since most have been met in this study such as review of the curricular content, establishment of a theoretical base, prior formative research, use of both quantitative and qualitative methods, evidence from a large number of classrooms, use of a broad set of instruments, comparative evidence of student achievement from quasi-experimental designs, detailed information about implementation, data from multiple sites for more than two years, and so forth.

However, there are at least three criteria that were not met in this study. First, we gathered no information on administrators, policy makers (particularly school board members), or parents about the implementation of MiC. We agree with the importance of this suggestion since these are critical persons whose judgments about the utility of the materials can make a difference in long-term acceptance of the program. Second, we gathered no data on the cost of the implementing MiC in classrooms, nor did we gather comparative cost data for the use of conventional materials. While our primary interest in the study was about improved student achievement, we recognize that costs can be a determining factor as to whether a standards-based program is adopted and maintained.

Finally, we understand, but disagree, that evaluations must be confirmed by researchers unrelated to the developers of the curriculum. MiC was the joint product of two long-established research centers in an effort to develop and study the impact of new standards-based materials on the teaching and learning of mathematics. Initially, we saw the creation of the materials as research tools. For example, prior to the development of MiC, the Dutch developed two instructional units for high-school classes, and we jointly studied their use in classrooms. Neither unit became part of MiC (de Lange, J., Burrill, G., Romberg, T., & van Reeuwijk, M., 1993). In fact, the most important use of the various instructional units has been in the study of student understanding (Fennema & Romberg, 1999; Romberg, Carpenter, & Dremock, 2005), of the problems teachers face in changing their instructional practices (Romberg, 1997), and in particular, the study of classroom assessment practices (Romberg, 2004b). In fact, this study was not done primarily to determine if MiC was ready for wide-scale use. Instead, we viewed this summative evaluation as the natural next step in studying the process of implementation of the experimental units in classrooms. While we understand the inherent bias when persons involved in the development of the program evaluate it, we were aware of this problem, and at every step as experienced researchers tried to be objective about the information we collected, analyzed, and reported. We presented the research design, development of the composite indices, and preliminary findings at research conferences for review by other researchers, and we had an external reviewer who examined our analyses from pilot-testing of instruments to preliminary findings. Furthermore, there were extensive discussions of the design and analysis plan when Professor Romberg was a fellow at the Center for Advanced Study in the Behavioral Sciences in 1999–2000.

Conclusion

The complexity of instructional issues involved in creating and sustaining classrooms that support mathematical achievement with understanding include the interconnected roles of tasks; student–teacher interactions involving mathematics concepts; the reasonable, appropriate, and flexible use of technological tools in the classroom; classroom norms of collaborative and individual work; sustained professional development and teacher community; enhanced organizational support; and community and parent involvement and education. Implementing this reform vision of student achievement should mean, at a minimum, that students become mathematically literate.

To the extent that our research supports this vision, we conclude that Realistic Mathematics Education as exemplified in *Mathematics in Context* is a viable instructional approach that produces a high level of learning when implemented well.

References

Asher, H. B. (1976). *Causal modeling. Sage University Paper Series on Quantitative Applications in the Social Sciences*, (No. 07-003). Beverly Hills, CA: Sage.

Beaton, A. E., Mullis, I. V., Martin, M. O., Gonzalez, E. J., Kelly, D. L., & Smith, T. A. (1996). *Mathematics achievement in the middle school years: IEA's third international mathematics and science study (TIMSS)*. Chestnut Hill, MA: International Association for the Evaluation of Educational Achievement.

Biggs, J. B., & Collis, K. F. (1982). *Evaluating the quality of learning: The SOLO taxonomy (structure of observed learning outcomes)*. New York: Academic Press.

Brown, A. L. (1992). Theoretical and methodological challenges in evaluating complex interventions in classroom settings. *The Journal of Learning Sciences*, 2(2), 141–178.

Burkhardt, H. (2006). From design research to large-scale impact (Engineering research in education). In Akker, J. J. H. van den (Ed.), *Educational Design Research* (pp. 133–162). London: Routledge.

Campbell, D. T., & Stanley, J. C. (1963). Experimental and quasi-experimental designs for research on teaching. In N. L. Gage (Ed.), *Handbook of research on teaching* (pp. 171–246). Chicago: Rand McNally.

Carpenter, T. P., & Lehrer, R. (1999). Teaching and learning mathematics with understanding. In E. Fennema & T. A. Romberg (Eds.), *Classrooms that promote mathematical understanding* (pp. 19–32). Mahwah, NJ: Erlbaum.

Clarke, D. J. (1989). *Mathematical behavior and the transition from primary to secondary school*. Unpublished doctoral dissertation, Monash University.

Clements, D. H. (2007). Curriculum research: Toward a framework for "research-based" curricula. *Journal for Research in Mathematics Education*, 28(1), 35–70.

Collis, K., & Romberg, T. (1992). *Mathematical problem-solving profiles*. Melbourne, Australia: Australian Council for Educational Research.

Cox, D. R. (1958). *Planning of experiments*. New York: Wiley.

CTB/McGraw-Hill. (1992). *California achievement test* (5th ed.). Monterey, CA: Author.

CTB/McGraw-Hill. (1997). *TerraNova*. Monterey, CA: Author.

Dekker, T., Querelle, N., van Reeuwijk, M., Wijers, M., Fejis, E., de Lange, J., Shafer, M. C., Davis, J., Wagner, L., Webb, D. (1997–1998). *Problem solving assessment system*. Madison, WI: University of Wisconsin.

de Lange, J., Burrill, G., Romberg, T., & van Reeuwijk, M. (1993). *Learning and testing mathematics in context*. Pleasantview, NY: Wings for Learning.

de Lange, J., van Reeuwijk, M., Feijs, E., Middleton, J. A., & Pligge, M. A. (1997). Figuring all the angles. In National Center for Research in Mathematical Sciences Education & Freudenthal Institute (Eds.), *Mathematics in context*. Chicago: Encyclopaedia Britannica.

DeNardo, J. (1998). Complexity, formal methods, and ideology in international studies. In M. Doyle & G. Ikenberry (Eds.), *New thinking in international relations theory*. New York: Westview Press.

Dossey, J., Mullis, I., Gorman, S., & Latham, A. (1994). *How school mathematics functions: Perspectives from the NAEP 1990 and 1992 assessments* (Report No. 23-FR-02). Washington, DC: Office of Educational Research and Improvement.

Fennema, E., & Romberg, T. A. (1999). *Mathematics classrooms that promote understanding*. Mahwah, NJ: Lawrence Erlbaum.

Feuer, M. J., Towne, L., & Shavelson, R. J. (2002) Scientific culture and educational research. *Educational Researcher*, 31(8), 4–14.

Freudenthal, H. (1983). *Didactical phenomenology of mathematical structures*. Dordrecht, The Netherlands: D. Reidel.

Freudenthal, H. (1987). Mathematics starting and staying in reality. In I. Wirszup & R. Street (Eds.), *Proceedings of the USCMP conference on mathematics education on development in school mathematics education around the world*. Reston, VA: National Council of Teachers of Mathematics.

Galen, F. van, Heuvel-Panhuisen, M. van den, & Pligge, M. A. (1998). Number tools. In National Center for Research in Mathematical Sciences Education & Freudenthal Institute (Eds.), *Mathematics in context*. Chicago, IL: Encyclopaedia Britannica.

Gravemeijer, K., Boswinkel, Meyer, M. R., & Shew, J. A. (1997). Measure for measure. In National Center for Research in Mathematical Sciences Education & Freudenthal Institute (Eds.), *Mathematics in context*. Chicago: Encyclopaedia Britannica.

Gravemeijer, K., Roodhardt, A., Wijers, M., Cole, B. R., & Burrill, G. (1998). Expressions and formulas. In National Center for Research in Mathematical Sciences Education & Freudenthal Institute (Eds.), *Mathematics in context*. Chicago: Encyclopaedia Britannica.

Harcourt Brace Educational Measurement. (1997). *Stanford mathematics achievement test (SAT)* (9th ed.). San Antonio, TX: Harcourt Brace.

Hayduk, L. A. (1987). *Structural equation modeling with LISREL*. Baltimore, MD: The Johns Hopkins University Press.

Heise, D. R. (1975). *Causal analysis*. New York: John Wiley.

Keijzer, R., Heuvel-Panhuisen, M. van den, Wijers, M., Shew, J. A., Brinker, L., Pligge, M. A., Shafer, M. C., & Brendefur, J. (1998). More or less. In National Center for Research in Mathematical Sciences Education & Freudenthal Institute (Eds.), *Mathematics in context*. Chicago, IL: Encyclopaedia Britannica.

Kilpatrick, J., Swafford, J., & Findell, B. (2001). *Adding it up: Helping children learn mathematics*. Washington, DC: National Academy Press.

Lagemann, E. C. (2000). *An elusive science: The troubling history of education research*. Chicago: University of Chicago Press.

Lagemann, E. C., & Shulman, L. S. (1999). *Issues in education research: Problems and possibilities*. San Francisco: Jossey-Bass.

Ma, X., & Kishor, N. (1997). Assessing the relationship between attitude toward mathematics and achievement in mathematics: A meta-analysis. *Journal for Research in Mathematics Education*, (28), 26–47.

Masters, G. (1982). A Rasch model for partial credit scoring. *Psychometrika*, 47(2), 149–174.

Masters, G., & Forster, M. (1996). *Progress maps*. Melbourne, Australia: Australian Council for Educational Research.

McLeod, D. B. (1992). Research on affect in mathematics education: A reconceptualization. In D. A. Grouws (Ed.), *Handbook of research on mathematics teaching and learning*. NY: Macmillan.

National Center for Research in Mathematical Sciences Education & Freudenthal Institute (Eds.). (1997–1998). *Mathematics in context*. Chicago: Encyclopaedia Britannica.

National Council of Teachers of Mathematics. (1989). *Curriculum and evaluation standards for school mathematics*. Reston, VA: Author.

National Council of Teachers of Mathematics. (1991). *Professional standards for teaching mathematics*. Reston, VA: Author.

National Council of Teachers of Mathematics. (1995). *Assessment standards for school mathematics*. Reston, VA: Author.

National Research Council. (2004). *On evaluating curricular effectiveness: Judging the quality of K-12 mathematics evaluations*. Washington, DC: Mathematical Sciences Education Board, Center for Education, Division of Behavioral and Social Sciences and Education, The National Academy Press.

Newmann, F. M., King, M. B., Youngs, P. (Draft, 2000, May). *Professional development that addresses school capacity: Lessons from urban elementary schools*. Paper presented at the annual meeting of the American Educational Research Association, New Orleans.

Newmann, F. M., Secada, W. G., & Wehlage, G. G. (1995). *A guide to authentic instruction and assessment: Vision, standards, and scoring*. Madison, WI: Wisconsin Center for Education Research.

Noss, R., & Hoyles, C. (1996). *Windows on mathematical meanings: Learning cultures and computers*. Dordrecht, The Netherlands: Kluwer.

Organisation for Economic Co-Operation and Development. (1999). *Measuring student knowledge and skills: A new framework for assessment*. Paris: OECD Publications.

Popkewitz, T. S., Tabachnick, B. R., & Wehlage, G. G. (1982). *The myth of educational reform: A study of school responses to a program of change*. Madison, WI: University of Wisconsin Press.

President's Committee of Advisors on Science and Technology-Panel on Educational Technology. (1997). *Report to the president on the use of technology to strengthen K-12 education in the United States*. Washington, DC: Author.

Rasch, G. (1960). *Probabilistic models for some intelligence and attainment tests*. Copenhagen: Danish Institute of Education.

Romberg, T. A. (Ed.). (1985). *Toward effective schooling: The IGE experience*. Washington, DC: University Press of America.

Romberg, T. A. (1987). A causal model to monitor changes in school mathematics.

In T. A. Romberg and D. Stewart (Eds.), *The monitoring of school mathematics: Background papers*, Vol. 1. (pp. 63–79). Madison, WI: Wisconsin Center for Education Research.

Romberg, T. A. (1988). *Evaluation: A coat of many colors.* A paper presented to Theme Group-T-4 "Evaluation and Assessment" at the Sixth International Congress on Mathematical Education, Budapest, Hungary,

Romberg, T. A. (1992). Perspectives on scholarship and research methods. In D. A. Grouws, (Ed.), *Handbook of research on mathematics teaching and learning*, (pp. 49–64). New York: Macmillan.

Romberg, T. A. (1997). Mathematics in context: Impact on teachers. In E. Fennema & B. S. Nelson, *Mathematics teachers in transition*. Mahwah, NJ: Erlbaum.

Romberg, T. A. (2001). *Designing middle-school mathematics materials using problems set in context to help students progress from informal to formal mathematical reasoning.* Madison, WI: Wisconsin Center for Education Research.

Romberg, T. A. (2004a). *Research methods for classroom studies.* Madison, WI: Wisconsin Center for Education Research.

Romberg, T. A. (2004b). *Standards-based mathematics assessment in middle-school.* New York: Teachers College Press.

Romberg, T. A. (2004c). Standards-based reform and *Mathematics in Context.* In T. A. Romberg, & M. C. Shafer (Eds.), *Purpose, plans, goals, and conduct of the study.* (Longitudinal/ Cross-Sectional Study of the Impact of Teaching Mathematics using *Mathematics in Context* on Student Achievement: Monograph 1), 7–17. Madison, WI: University of Wisconsin–Madison.

Romberg, T. A., Carpenter, T. P., & Dremock, F. (2005). *Understanding mathematics and science matters.* Mahwah, NJ: Lawrence Erlbaum.

Romberg, T. A., & Shafer, M. C. (2004a). Background information on students at the start of the study. In T. A. Romberg, M. C. Shafer, & L. Folgert (Eds.), *Background on students and teachers.* (Longitudinal/Cross-Sectional Study of the Impact of Teaching Mathematics using *Mathematics in Context* on Student Achievement: Monograph 2), 7–68. Madison, WI: University of Wisconsin–Madison.

Romberg, T. A., & Shafer, M. C. (2004b). The design of the longitudinal/cross-sectional study. In T. A. Romberg, & M. C. Shafer (Eds.), *Purpose, plans, goals, and conduct of the study.* (Longitudinal/Cross-Sectional Study of the Impact of Teaching Mathematics using *Mathematics in Context* on Student Achievement: Monograph 1), 18–30. Madison, WI: University of Wisconsin–Madison.

Romberg, T. A., & Shafer, M. C. (2005). What we have learned. In T. A. Romberg, & M. C. Shafer (Eds.), *Implications and conclusions* (Longitudinal/Cross-Sectional Study of the Impact of Teaching Mathematics using *Mathematics in Context* on Student Achievement: Monograph 8), 65–83. Madison, WI: University of Wisconsin–Madison.

Romberg, T. A., Shafer, M. C., Folgert, L., Balakul, S., Lee, C., & Kwako, J. (2004). Information on teacher background variables. In T. A. Romberg, M. C. Shafer, & L. Folgert (Eds.), *Background on students and teachers.* (Longitudinal/Cross-Sectional Study of the Impact of Teaching Mathematics using *Mathematics in Context* on Student Achievement: Monograph 2), 69–85. Madison, WI: University of Wisconsin–Madison.

Romberg, T. A., Shafer, M. C., Folgert, L., & LeMire, S. (2005a). Other results. In T. A. Romberg, M. C. Shafer, & L. Folgert (Eds.), *Differences in student performance for three treatment groups* (Longitudinal/Cross-Sectional Study of the Impact of Teaching Mathematics using *Mathematics in Context* on Student Achievement: Monograph 7) 112–143. Madison, WI: University of Wisconsin–Madison.

Romberg, T. A., Shafer, M. C., Webb, D. C., & Folgert, L. (Eds.). (2005b). *Differences in performance between Mathematics in Context and conventional students.* (Longitudinal/Cross-Sectional Study of the Impact of Teaching Mathematics using *Mathematics in Context* on Student Achievement: Monograph 6). Madison, WI: University of Wisconsin–Madison.

Romberg, T. A., Shafer, M. C., Webb, D. C., & Folgert, L. (Eds.). (2005c). *The impact of MiC on student achievement.* (Longitudinal/Cross-Sectional Study of the Impact of Teaching Mathematics using *Mathematics in Context* on Student Achievement: Monograph 5). Madison, WI: University of Wisconsin–Madison.

Romberg, T. A. & Wilson, J. W. (1972). Patterns of mathematical achievement in grade 12. *NLSMA Report No. 18.* Stanford, CA: SMSG.

SAS Institute. (2000). *SAS* (9th ed.). Cary, NC: Author.

Schmidt, W. H., McKnight, C. C., Houang, R. T., Wang, H., Wiley, D. E., Cogan, L. S., & Wolfe, R. G. (2001). *Why schools matter: A cross-national comparison of curriculum and learning.* San Francisco, CA: Jossey-Bass.

Schoenfeld, A. H. (1994). A discourse on methods [25th Anniversary Special Issue]. *Journal for Research in Mathematics Education*, 25(6), 697–710.

Schoenfeld, A. H. (2001). Mathematics education in the 20th century. In L. Corno (Ed.), *Education across a century: The centennial volume: Part I. 100th yearbook of the National Society for the Study of Education.* Chicago: University of Chicago Press.

Shafer, M. C. (1999). *Student questionnaire: Transition into high school* (Technical Report No. 55). Madison, WI: University of Wisconsin–Madison.

Shafer, M. C. (2004a). Conduct of the study. In T. A. Romberg, & M. C. Shafer (Eds.), *Purpose, plans, goals, and conduct of the study.* (Longitudinal/Cross-Sectional Study of the Impact of Teaching Mathematics using *Mathematics in Context* on Student Achievement: Monograph 1), 51–93. Madison, WI: University of Wisconsin–Madison.

Shafer, M. C. (2004b). Instrumentation, sampling, and operational plan. In T. A. Romberg & M. C. Shafer (Eds.), *Purpose, plans, goals, and conduct of the study.* (Longitudinal/Cross-Sectional Study of the Impact of Teaching Mathematics using *Mathematics in Context* on Student Achievement: Monograph 1), 31–50. Madison, WI: University of Wisconsin–Madison.

Shafer, M. C. (2005a). The quality of instruction. In M. C. Shafer, *Instruction, opportunity to learn with understanding, and school capacity.* (Longitudinal/Cross-Sectional Study of the Impact of Teaching Mathematics using *Mathematics in Context* on Student Achievement: Monograph 3), 10–52. Madison, WI: University of Wisconsin–Madison.

Shafer, M. C. (2005b). Opportunity to learn with understanding. In M. C. Shafer, *Instruction, opportunity to learn with understanding, and school capacity.* (Longitudinal/Cross-Sectional Study of the Impact of Teaching Mathematics using

Mathematics in Context on Student Achievement: Monograph 3), 53–80. Madison, WI: University of Wisconsin–Madison.

Shafer, M. C. (2005c). School capacity. In M. C. Shafer, *Instruction, opportunity to learn with understanding, and school capacity*. (Longitudinal/Cross-Sectional Study of the Impact of Teaching Mathematics using *Mathematics in Context* on Student Achievement: Monograph 3), 81–101. Madison, WI: University of Wisconsin–Madison.

Shafer, M. C., Davis, J., & Wagner, L. R. (1997a). *Principal interview: School context*. (Longitudinal/Cross-Sectional Study of the Impact of Teaching Mathematics using *Mathematics in Context* on Student Achievement: Working Paper No. 12). Madison, WI: University of Wisconsin–Madison.

Shafer, M. C., Davis, J., & Wagner, L. R. (1997b). *Teacher interview: Teaching and learning mathematics*. (Longitudinal/Cross-Sectional Study of the Impact of Teaching Mathematics using *Mathematics in Context* on Student Achievement: Working Paper No. 4). Madison, WI: University of Wisconsin–Madison.

Shafer, M. C., Davis, J., & Wagner, L. R. (1997c). *Teacher questionnaire: Professional opportunities*. (Longitudinal/Cross-Sectional Study of the Impact of Teaching Mathematics using *Mathematics in Context* on Student Achievement: Working Paper No. 11). Madison, WI: University of Wisconsin–Madison.

Shafer, M. C., Davis, J., & Wagner, L. R. (1997d). *Teacher questionnaire: School context*. (Longitudinal/Cross-Sectional Study of the Impact of Teaching Mathematics using *Mathematics in Context* on Student Achievement: Working Paper No. 10). Madison, WI: University of Wisconsin–Madison.

Shafer, M. C., Davis, J., & Wagner, L. R. (1998). *Teacher interview: Instructional planning and classroom interaction*. (Longitudinal/Cross-Sectional Study of the Impact of Teaching Mathematics using *Mathematics in Context* on Student Achievement: Working Paper No. 3). Madison, WI: University of Wisconsin–Madison.

Shafer, M. C., Romberg, T. A., & Folgert, L. (2005). Classroom achievement of comparable classes. In T. A. Romberg, M. C. Shafer, & L. Folgert (Eds.), *Differences in student performance for the three treatment groups*. (Longitudinal/Cross-Sectional Study of the Impact of Teaching Mathematics using *Mathematics in Context* on Student Achievement: Monograph 7), 8–38. Madison, WI: University of Wisconsin–Madison.

Shafer, M. C., Wagner, L. R., & Davis, J. (1997a). *Classroom observation scale*. (Longitudinal/Cross-Sectional Study of the Impact of Teaching Mathematics using *Mathematics in Context* on Student Achievement: Working Paper No. 6). Madison, WI: University of Wisconsin–Madison.

Shafer, M. C., Wagner, L. R., & Davis, J. (1997b). *Student attitude inventory*. (Longitudinal/Cross-Sectional Study Working Paper No. 7). Madison, WI: University of Wisconsin, Wisconsin Center for Education Research.

Shafer, M. C., Wagner, L. R., & Davis, J. (1997c). *Teaching log*. (Longitudinal/Cross-Sectional Study of the Impact of Teaching Mathematics using *Mathematics in Context* on Student Achievement: Working Paper No. 5). Madison, WI: University of Wisconsin–Madison.

Shavelson, R., & Towne, L. (Eds.). (2002). *Scientific inquiry in education*. Washington, DC: National Academy Press.

Stewart, J., Cartier, J., & Passmore, C. (2001). *Scientific practice as a context for inquiry and argumentation in science classrooms* (Project MUSE Position Paper). Madison: University of Wisconsin–Madison, National Center for the Improvement of Student Learning and Achievement in Mathematics and Science.

Turner, R., & O'Connor, G. (2005). The development of a single scale for mapping progress in mathematical competence. In T. A. Romberg, D. C. Webb, M. C. Shafer, & L. Folgert (Eds.), *Measures of student performance*. (Longitudinal/Cross-Sectional Study of the Impact of Teaching Mathematics using *Mathematics in Context* on Student Achievement: Monograph 4), 27–66. Madison, WI: University of Wisconsin–Madison.

Walker, D. F. (1992). Methodological issues in curriculum research. In P. W. Jackson (Ed.), *Handbook of research on curriculum* (pp. 98–118). New York: Macmillan.

Webb, D. C., Romberg, T. A., Shafer, M. C., & Wagner, L. R. (2005). Classroom achievement. In T. A. Romberg, D. C. Webb, M. C. Shafer, & L. Folgert (Eds.), *Measures of student performance*. (Longitudinal/Cross-Sectional Study of the Impact of Teaching Mathematics using *Mathematics in Context* on Student Achievement: Monograph 4), 7–26. Madison, WI: University of Wisconsin–Madison.

Wijers, M., Roodhardt, A., van Reeuwijk, M., Burrill, G., Cole, B., & Pligge, M. A. (1998). Building formulas. In National Center for Research in Mathematical Sciences Education & Freudenthal Institute (Eds.), *Mathematics in context*. Chicago, IL: Encyclopaedia Britannica.

Index

Analysis of covariance 120–3, 134
Analysis of variance 119–20
Application 10, 127, 128, 157, 165, 171
Asher, H. B. 9
Assessment 2, 12, 27, 140, 152, 168
Assessments designed for the study
19, 24, 29, 47, 51, 56–8, 62–3, 80,
81, 82, 85, 87, 113, 114, 115, 116,
120, 132, 162, 164, 169, 171; *see
also* External Assessment System,
Problem Solving Assessment
Attitudes 10, 61, 127, 128, 131, 135,
137, 157
Attrition 25, 69, 80, 95, 101, 162, 164,
169
Australian Council for Educational
Research 58, 159

Balakul, S. 36, 132, 135, 155
Beaton, A. E. 61
Bias 5, 8, 90
Biggs, J. B. 62, 135
Boswinkel, N. 41
Brendefur, J. 28
Brinker, L. 28
Brown, A. L. 3
Burkhardt, H. 2
Burrill, G. 30, 42, 54, 174

Campbell, D. T. 5, 18
Carpenter, T. P. 29, 49, 174
Cartier, J. 7
Causal paths 18, 19
Clarke, D. J. 131
Classroom achievement index (CA)
13, 39, 58, 59, 60, 61, 63, 64–89,
97–126, 127, 128, 129, 130, 132–5,
136, 137, 139, 141, 143, 144, 146,
147, 148, 149, 152, 157, 159, 160,
165, 171, 173
Classroom assessment practice 28, 29,
30, 31, 35, 38, 39, 40, 41, 91, 140,
143, 144–5, 163, 174
Classroom Events 10, 140, 142–4, 148,
150, 157, 159, 172
Classroom observation instrument
19, 23, 39, 161, 163
Classroom observations 16, 19, 22,
24, 28, 29, 30, 51, 91, 162, 163
Clements, D. H. 2
Cogan, L. S. 155
Cole, B. R. 30, 42, 54
Collis, K. 24, 61, 62, 135
*Collis-Romberg Mathematical
Problem Solving Profiles* 24, 61–2,
135, 137, 138
Commitment 87, 162, 163, 164
Composite variables 13, 39, 91, 127,
131, 140, 141, 156, 159, 160
Conceptual understanding 28, 40, 42,
43, 51, 52, 53, 54, 55, 90, 91, 92, 93,
97, 103, 124, 147, 148, 153, 154,
163, 166
Consequent variables 10, 13, 127, 158
Conventional treatment group
94–113, 119–24, 124–6, 131, 134,
166, 171
Cox, D. R. 4
Cronbach, Lee 2
Cross-grade comparisons 64, 69–75,
76, 101–5, 160
Cross-sectional comparisons 19, 64,
69, 74, 89, 97, 169
Cross-year comparisons 64, 75–80,
87, 105–13, 160
CTB/McGraw-Hill 60, 119

Curricular Content and Materials 10,
  51–2, 55, 92, 140, 147, 148, 172, 173

Davis, J. 24, 39, 45, 57, 61, 128
Dekker, T. 57
de Lange, J. 53, 57, 174
DeNardo, J. 3
Dossey, J. 61
Dremock, F. 174

Encyclopaedia Britannica 29
Experimental method 3
Experimental units 4, 5, 6, 7, 90, 92,
  93, 94, 95, 160, 170
Experiments, true 7, 90, 160
External Assessment System 33, 56–7,
  58, 81, 113, 123, 127–8, 137

Feijs, E. 53, 57
Fennema, E. 174
Feuer, M. J. 1
Findell, B. 1
Folgert, L. 34, 36, 43, 47, 50, 51, 64,
  90, 97, 120, 124, 132, 134, 135, 137,
  151, 155
Forster, M. 58
Freudenthal, Hans 15, 16
Freudenthal Institute 57
Further Pursuits 10, 131, 157, 171

Galen, F. van 28
Gonzalez, E. J. 61
Gorman, S. 61
Grade-level-by-year studies 19, 64–9,
  74, 87, 89, 94, 97–101, 114, 127,
  128, 129, 130, 137, 160, 173
Gravemeijer, K. 41, 42, 54

Harcourt Brace Educational
  Measurement 60, 119
Hayduk, L. A. 9
Heise, D. R. 9
Heuvel-Panhiusen, M. van den 28
Houang, R. T. 155
Hoyles, C. 170

Implementing curricular materials 2,
  7, 14, 15, 16, 17, 18, 20, 21, 23, 29,
  33, 34, 37, 43, 44, 51, 93, 94, 158,
  160, 163, 167, 173, 174
Implementing *Mathematics in
  Context* 29, 33, 37, 43, 47, 82, 85,

87, 89, 113, 123, 124, 125, 126, 134,
  148, 149, 152, 153–4, 157, 160, 162,
  163, 165, 166–7, 173, 174
Independent variables 10, 13, 127,
  140, 158
Index (indices) 12, 13, 39, 40, 51, 58,
  91, 119, 128, 157, 159, 161, 163, 174
Indicators 12, 13, 39, 51, 91
Instruction 2, 3, 6, 7, 8, 10, 12, 13, 16,
  17, 27, 39, 49, 90, 96, 147, 152, 155,
  159, 166, 168, 172, 173, 174
Instruction index 13, 39–44, 67, 69,
  70, 72, 74, 87, 91–2, 93, 94, 97, 101,
  119, 124, 125, 126, 127, 140–7, 152,
  157, 159, 160, 161, 165, 172
Item Response Theory 59
Intervening variables 10, 13, 127, 140,
  141, 147, 158, 172
Interviews 19, 24, 30, 39, 40, 45, 51,
  91, 95, 153, 154, 155, 156, 170, 172

Journal entries 40, 51, 91, 153, 154,
  156, 161, 172

Keijzer, R. 28
Kelly, D. L. 61
Kilpatrick, J. 1
King, M. B. 44
Kishor, N. 61
Knowledge and Understanding 10, 127,
  128, 157, 165, 171
Kwako, J. 36, 132, 135, 155

Lagemann, E. C. 2
Latham, A. 61
Learning mathematics with
  understanding 34, 164, 165
Lee, C. 36, 132, 135
Lehrer, R. 29, 49
LeMire, S. 120, 135
Longitudinal comparisons 17, 19, 22,
  64, 80–7, 89, 97, 113–19, 135, 158,
  159, 160, 162, 164, 169, 170

Ma, X. 61
Martin, M. O. 61
Masters, G. 58, 59
Mathematics in Context (MiC) 2, 9,
  12, 14, 15, 16, 17, 18, 19, 20, 21, 22,
  23, 24, 26, 28, 29, 34, 35, 37, 49, 50,
  55, 108, 121, 127, 147, 148, 149,
  158, 164, 166, 173, 174

McKnight, C. C. 155
McLeod, D. B. 61
Meyer, M. R. 41
MiC (Conventional) treatment group
    93, 94–113, 119–24, 124–6, 134, 171
MiC instructional approach 9, 17, 56,
    64–89, 108, 113, 123, 126, 166, 171,
    174
MiC treatment group 93, 94, 119–24,
    124–6, 131, 134, 171
Middleton, J. A. 53
Moses, Lincoln 13
Mullis, I. 61

National Assessment of Educational
    Progress (NAEP) 56, 128
National Council of Teachers of
    Mathematics 1, 15, 27, 81
National Research Council 173
National Science Foundation (NSF)
    1, 15, 19, 20, 21, 160, 161, 162, 171
Newmann, F. M. 29, 44
Noss, R. 170

O'Connor, G. 58, 128, 160
Opportunity to learn 22, 39, 48, 49,
    51, 148
Opportunity to learn with
    understanding 16, 17, 43, 49, 50,
    51, 158, 172
Opportunity to learn with
    understanding (OTLu) index 13,
    39, 51–5, 69, 70, 72, 74, 87, 89, 91,
    92–3, 94, 101, 119, 124, 125, 126,
    127, 140, 147–50, 152, 157, 159,
    160, 165, 172
Organisation for Economic Co-
    Operation and Development 59
Outcome variables 10, 13, 127

Passmore, C. 7
Pedagogical Decisions 10, 140, 142,
    143, 157, 172
Pligge, M. A. 28, 30, 53
Popkewitz, T. S. 8
President's Committee of Advisors
    on Science and Technology 1
Prior achievement 132, 159
Prior achievement index 13, 39, 60,
    66, 67, 72, 87, 89, 95, 96, 97, 101,
    119–26, 127, 132–5, 137, 157, 159,
    165

Prior variables 10, 13, 127, 132, 158
Problem Solving Assessment System
    24, 27, 31, 33, 56, 57–8, 81, 113,
    120, 121, 122, 123, 128, 137
Professional development 24, 27,
    33–4, 35, 36, 46, 55, 140, 151, 152,
    156, 162, 163, 168, 170, 174
Professional development institutes
    19, 23, 24, 27–33, 35, 156, 166
Program for International Student
    Assessment (PISA) 59, 60
Progress maps 58–60, 160

Qualitative methods 3, 13, 18, 154,
    170, 173
Quantitative methods 3, 13, 18, 173
Quasi-experimental research design 5,
    18, 20, 90, 160, 173
Querelle, N. 57

Randomized experiments 2, 3, 5, 7,
    18, 60, 90, 171
Rasch, G. 59
Realistic Mathematics Education 15,
    174
Reeuwijk, M. van 30, 53, 174
Reform-based curriculum 18, 30, 51,
    153; see also standards-based
    curriculum
Research-based curriculum 1, 172
Research design of the studies 11, 13,
    16–20, 21–5, 27, 29, 64, 127, 131,
    140, 156, 157, 158, 159, 167, 168,
    172–3, 174
Research instruments 19, 23, 27, 56,
    63, 157, 158, 159, 161, 167, 168,
    170, 171, 172, 173, 174
Research sites 22–3, 162–4, 168–9,
    172, 173
Romberg, T. A. 1, 2, 4, 10, 13, 15, 16,
    24, 28, 31, 34, 36, 43, 47, 50, 56, 57,
    59, 60, 61, 64, 90, 92, 97, 120, 124,
    127, 131, 132, 134, 135, 137, 151,
    155, 158, 171, 174
Roodhardt, A. 30, 42, 54

SAS 119
Scales 10, 12, 18
Schmidt, W. H. 155
Schoenfeld, A. H. 2
School capacity 39, 44, 47–8, 55, 149,
    159, 172

School capacity index 13, 44–7, 96, 97, 101, 119, 127, 140, 149–52, 157
School context 10, 14, 24, 72, 137
Secada, W. G. 29
Shafer, M. C. 10, 15, 19, 21, 24, 25, 27, 28, 31, 34, 36, 37, 39, 40, 43, 44, 45, 47, 49, 50, 56, 57, 61, 62, 64, 90, 92, 97, 120, 124, 127, 128, 131, 132, 134, 135, 137, 140, 147, 151, 153, 155, 158, 171
Shavelson, R. 1, 2
Shew, J. A. 28, 41
Shulman, L. S. 2
Smith, T. A. 61
Social context 10, 13, 69, 74, 101, 105, 108, 132
Standardized tests 24, 34, 46, 51, 56, 60, 62, 69, 74, 80, 92, 95, 119, 132, 134, 159, 163, 164, 166, 169, 172
Standards-based curriculum 1, 2, 5, 8, 14, 15, 16, 17, 20, 158, 164, 167, 170, 172, 173; see also reform-based curriculum
Stanley, J. C. 5, 18
Stewart, J. 7
Structural equations 127, 160, 173
Structural model 2, 7, 8, 9, 10, 12, 13, 17, 18, 20, 141, 142, 143, 151, 153, 157, 158, 159, 160, 172–3
Student Attitude Inventory 19, 23, 24, 61, 128, 170–1
Student Background 10, 72, 95, 132, 135, 137, 157, 159
Student Pursuits 10, 39, 91, 140, 143, 146, 147, 157, 172
Student questionnaire 19, 23, 24, 131, 132
Summative evaluation 1, 2, 3, 4, 5, 7, 8, 13, 14, 56, 158, 167, 171, 172, 173–4
Support Environment 10, 140, 151–2
Swafford, J. 1

Tabachnick, B. R. 8
Teacher Background 10, 36–7, 47, 96, 132, 140, 159
Teacher Knowledge 10, 140, 153–5, 157, 159, 170
Teacher logs 12, 19, 23, 24, 29, 30, 39, 40, 51, 91, 161, 162, 172
Teacher Professional Responsibility 10, 140, 153, 155–6, 170
Teacher questionnaires 19, 23, 36, 45, 51, 91, 154, 155, 156, 157, 170
Teaching mathematics for understanding 34, 40, 48, 49, 51, 53, 54, 55, 66, 70, 72, 87, 91, 92, 101, 126, 141, 142, 147, 148, 149, 150, 159, 161, 164
TIMSS 56, 128
Towne, L. 1, 2
Treatment fidelity 16, 36, 37–9, 44, 47, 164
Treatment groups 90–4, 159, 160, 172; see also Conventional treatment group; MiC (Conventional) group; and MiC treatment group
Turner, R. 58, 128, 160

Unit of analysis 12, 18, 120, 160, 173

Variables 3, 7, 9, 10, 12, 13, 17, 18, 19, 23, 39, 51, 55, 60, 119, 120, 127, 153, 156, 158, 159, 160, 163, 172, 173

Wagner, L. R. 24, 31, 39, 45, 56, 57, 61, 128
Walker, D. F. 1
Wang, H. 155
Webb, D. C. 31, 43, 56, 57, 64, 90, 97, 132, 134, 137
Wehlage, G. G. 8, 29
Wijers, M. 28, 30, 42, 54, 57
Wiley, D. F. 155
Wilson, J. W. 1
Wolfe, R. G. 155

Youngs, P. 44